CURTAINS
—and—
WINDOW
TREATMENTS

CURTAINS
and
WINDOW
TREATMENTS

Angela Fishburn

VNR VAN NOSTRAND REINHOLD COMPANY
NEW YORK CINCINNATI TORONTO LONDON MELBOURNE

For my father

Library of Congress Catalog Card Number 82-23717

ISBN 0-442-22498-2

Printed in Great Britain

Published by Van Nostrand Reinhold Company Inc.
135 West 50th Street
New York, New York 10020

16 15 14 13 12 11 10 9 8 7 6 5 4 3 2 1

Library of Congress Cataloging in Publication Data

Fishburn, Angela.
  Curtains and window treatments.

  Includes index.
  1. Drapery. 2. Blinds. 3. Window-shades. I. Title.
TT390.F57 1983   646.2'1   82-23717
ISBN 0-442-22498-2

Contents

Introduction

Here is a book for those who would like to make their own curtains and blinds to a professional standard — and to dress their windows with style.

Well-planned window treatments do much to furnish a room, as together with floor and wall coverings they provide the greatest expanse of colour and texture. They are vitally important to the overall decor and atmosphere of a room and therefore deserve careful thought in their planning, design and construction.

I hope that this book will not only help with the techniques of making curtains and blinds, but will also suggest some fresh and interesting ways of treating all types of windows.

Acknowledgment

I should like to thank Katie Beckett for her help in reading the transcript. Thanks are also due to the suppliers of photographs, as follows: front jacket, Sanderson, back jacket, Mark Gerson. Colour photographs 1, 2 and 5, Sanderson; 3, CVP Designs; 4, Shand Kydd; 6, Crown Wallpapers; 7, Alma Rafter. Black and white photographs, pages 36 and 42, Palu & Lake; pages 44 and 76, Sanderson; pages 96 and 106, Rufflette. Finally, many thanks to Jackie Allen for the illustrations.

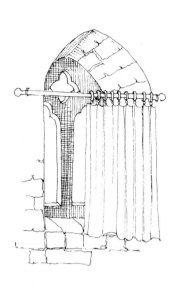

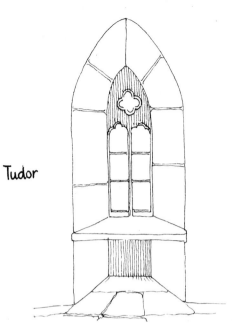

Tudor

Elizabethan

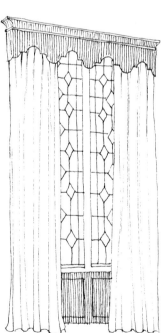
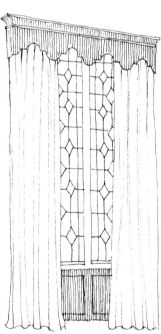

Jacobean

Regency

1
Choosing a Window Style

Windows are an important part of the architecture of a room and ideally should be dressed so that they are in keeping with its period, be it modern, Georgian or any other. Windows were originally designed to let in light, and as life through the ages became safer, windows became larger and lower and curtains began to play an important part in the furnishing scheme.

As well as contributing to the design of a room, curtains have two important functions — they provide privacy and comfort, and insulation against cold and noise. Insulation may not be important in a hot climate, or where there is double glazing, but in cooler climates and noisy cities it is comforting to have something to draw over the window. Fabric over windows can either be hung to pull sideways — as in traditional curtains, or hung to pull up — as in roller blinds, Roman blinds or festoon blinds.

Each window should be considered carefully before a treatment is decided upon. It must be part of the furnishings and should fit into the mood of the room — period or modern. Window dressing gives ample opportunity for original design.

No windows are average and most people have at least one 'problem' window to treat. There are many types of windows and all present different problems and need to be dressed in various ways according to their position and the effect that is required (figs 1—12).

Look at the room as a whole and decide on a particular style. Bear in mind the outlook from the windows and the lightness of the room. Secluded views and attractive gardens should be enjoyed to the full and the windows will need only a simple treatment. Bright attractive curtains or blinds, on the other hand, will liven up a dull or dark room or obscure an ugly view.

Many architectural shortcomings can be disguised,

if not remedied, by a clever use of curtains or blinds. Illusions of height, width and shape can be achieved if careful thought is given to the planning and treatment of windows and doors. It is necessary to find the right combination of track, fabric and style. Time is well spent in planning to achieve the desired effect.

An illusion of length or width can be obtained in many ways:

(a)   Use floor length curtains, or
(b)   Extend the pole or track several inches at each side of the window frame so that the curtains actually hang against the wall and well back from the window.
(c)   Have the pole or track well above the window to add to the height, perhaps using a valance or pelmet to disguise its shape.
(d)   If a window is considered too wide, the curtains may be hung inside the frame so that they hide part of the window.
(e)   Use of fabric with vertical stripes gives an illusion of height.

Café curtains can make a useful decorative feature where the view from the window is unattractive. They consist of one or two small pairs of curtains, one for the bottom half of the window and one for the top, the lower pair being suspended half way up the window. They are very versatile and can be most successful when used in kitchens and bathrooms.

It is important to consider whether the window is in proportion to the size of the room — is it too high or too low? For example, when an extension is added to a room this sometimes throws the original windows out of proportion. This situation can often be remedied successfully by an imaginative choice of curtains or blinds.

In a small room with low ceilings do not use curtains or blinds that will block out the light. The most

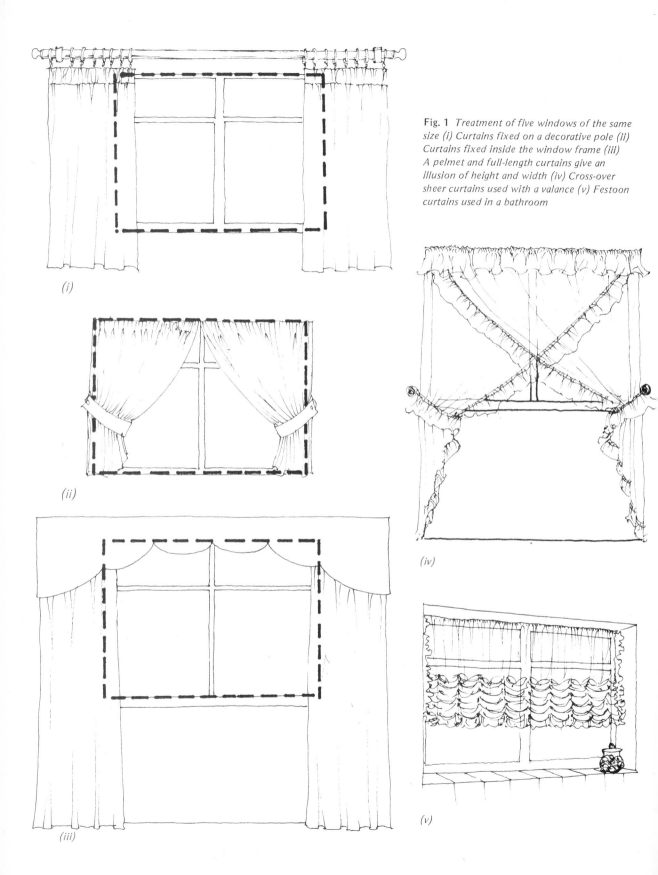

Fig. 1 *Treatment of five windows of the same size (i) Curtains fixed on a decorative pole (ii) Curtains fixed inside the window frame (iii) A pelmet and full-length curtains give an illusion of height and width (iv) Cross-over sheer curtains used with a valance (v) Festoon curtains used in a bathroom*

(i)

(ii)

(iii)

(iv)

(v)

(i)

Fig. 2 *Dormer window (i) Treating a dormer window with matching curtains, roller blind and window seat (ii) Roller blind with hand-painted motif (iii) Simple curtains used with tie-backs*

(ii)

(iii)

11

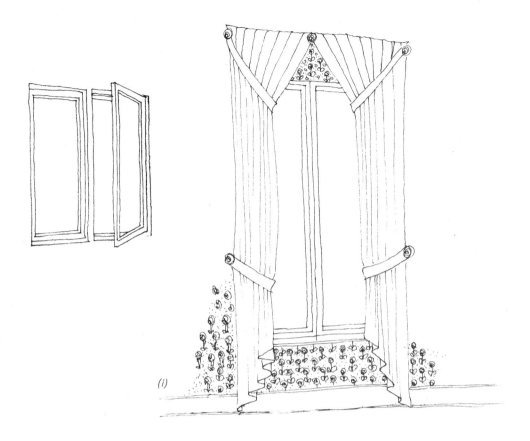

Fig. 3 *In-swinging window (i) Tie-backs used to keep the curtains away from an in-swinging window*

Fig. 4 *Four ways of treating strip windows*

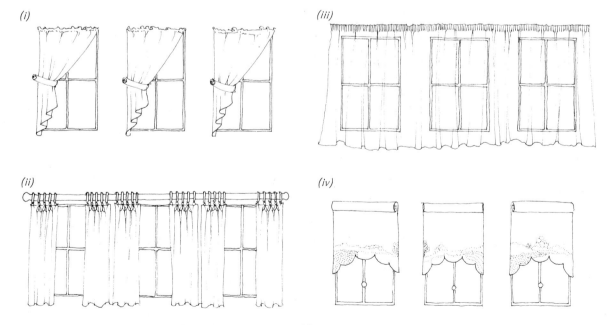

Fig. 5 *Arched window (i) Curtains cut and tailored to fit an arched window or doorway; although they cannot be drawn, the tie-back can be released to let the curtains fall free (ii) Pulling up curtains used on an arched window (iii) Tie-back used to hold curtains back at the side of a door (iv) and (v) A simple way of treating an arched window (vi) Flexible curtain track used round the arched section*

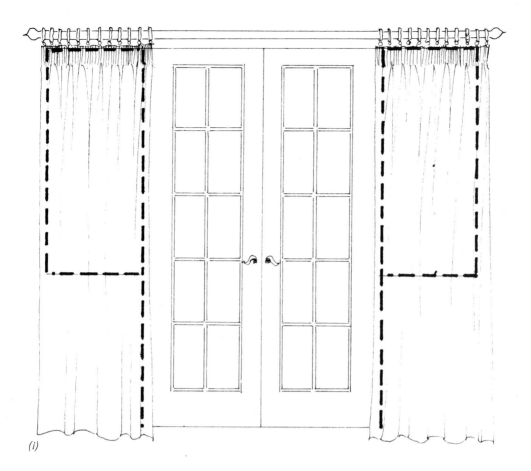

(i)

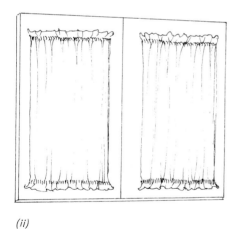

(ii)

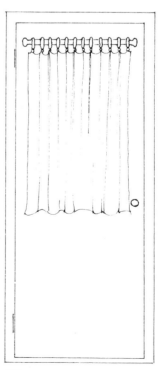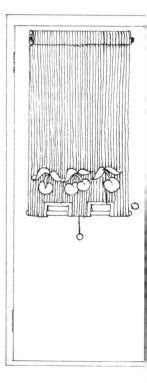

Fig. 6 *Doors (i) French window and doors treated as one unit
(ii) Sheer curtains held in place with rods at the top and
lower edges (iii) Two treatments of a half-glazed door
(iv) Treating a single door*

(iii)

(iv)

intense light enters a room from ceiling height, so choose a pole or track in this case and use a decorative heading on the curtains. Do not use pelmets or valances, for these would cut out some of this valuable light.

A large picture window from ceiling to floor obviously needs floor length curtains. Give these interest by using a decorative heading at the top of the curtains and perhaps braid or border on the leading edges. Avoid pelmets and valances and make sure that the track extends well beyond the window frame so that maximum advantage is taken of the large expanse of glass and the light it offers.

Bay windows and bow windows often present difficulties when their treatment is being planned. If possible, use one pair of full-length curtains. However, if it is necessary to have more than two curtains consider using a pelmet or valance to knit the unit together. Alternatively, use flexible track which can be bent round the curves, to let in maximum light.

Fig. 7 *Picture window in a bedroom treated with full-length curtains and a café curtain*

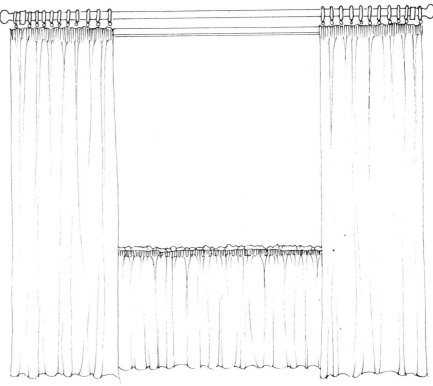

Fig. 8 *Bow windows (i) Café curtains give privacy in a bow window (ii) Curtains held back with double tie-backs (iii) Use of roller blinds with sheer curtains (iv) Café curtains in a bow window (v) Roman blinds used with dress curtains*

(i)

(ii)

(iii)

(iv)

(v)

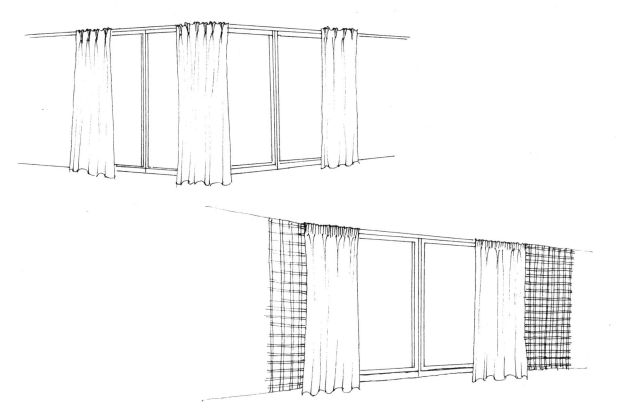

Fig. 9 *Sliding glass doors and patio windows; simple treatment ensures maximum light*

Fig. 10 *Corner windows*

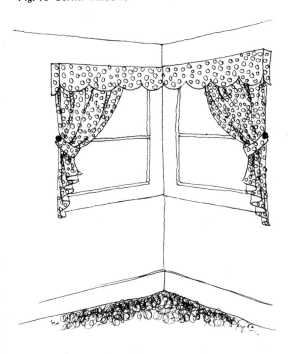

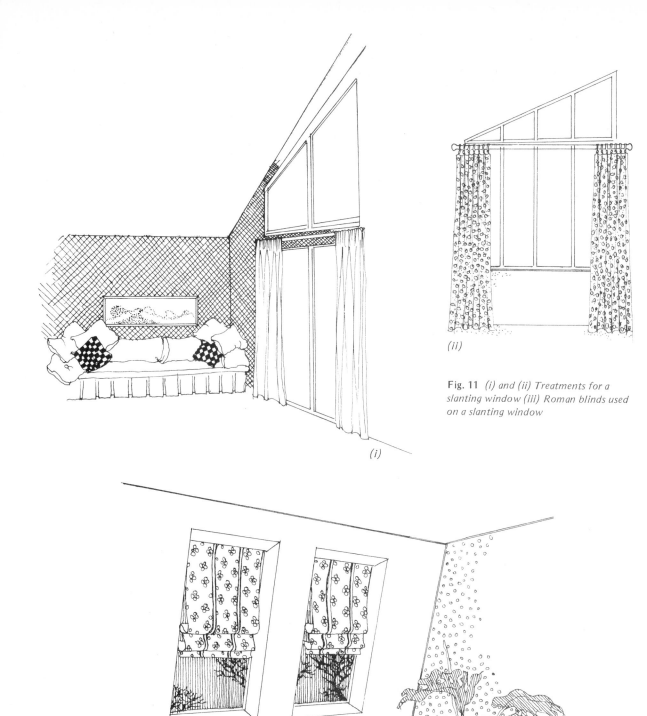

Fig. 11 *(i) and (ii) Treatments for a slanting window (iii) Roman blinds used on a slanting window*

(i)

(ii)

(iii)

Fig. 12 *Ways of treating a tall, narrow window*

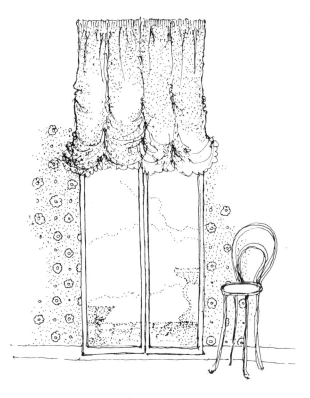

When there are two or three small windows along one wall, consider treating them as a whole, using one long track or pole. Arrange the curtains so that they cover the blank walls in the daytime. At night when the curtains are drawn, this type of treatment provides a large expanse of colour or texture instead of several small areas. A pelmet or valance could be used to link the whole together.

When treating a dormer window, consider using a roller blind and a small pair of dress curtains to match. These are fixed at the side of the windows and used purely for decoration. They cannot be drawn as they do not have enough width for actual use. If matching wallpaper is used for the surrounding alcove an attractive effect can be achieved.

Curved windows and archways might be treated by using a flexible track which can be bent to the shape of the window. Do not try to disguise an arched window; instead, make the most of its architectural features by cutting the curtains to fit it. The curtains are made to the full height of the windows and their tops gathered to the size required. They are then carefully cut to the curved line while gathered, and the heading is tailored to fit. Tie-backs need to be used with such curtains to hold them back as they cannot of course be drawn; they must be permanently fixed to the track. The tie-backs, however, can be released if required and the curtains allowed to fall free.

Floor length curtains look best in most rooms, but of course take more fabric. Short curtains can be used effectively in small rooms, but try to use long curtains in living rooms, dining rooms and main bedrooms.

Keep curtains as clean as possible by brushing and vacuuming them regularly. Do not let them become too soiled before having them dry cleaned or washed. One pair of curtains may have three different fabrics — face fabric, interlining and lining fabric — and each may need different cleaning techniques. If the curtains have hand-made headings they may also need specialist treatment and care.

The following treatments are useful when there is very little space at each side of the window to accommodate curtains:

(a) Roller blinds are economical to make and can be a very practical way of treating kitchen and bathroom windows, as they can be sponged clean. Roller blinds and café curtains can both be very effective when used with pelmets, valances or small dress curtains as this softens their rather hard line.

(b) A Roman blind is a flat piece of fabric that pulls upwards in pleats and is fixed to a wooden batten at the top of the window. These are similar to roller blinds, but instead of the fabric rolling on to a roller it is pleated up the window in folds. Tapes and rings are attached to the back of the fabric and cords are threaded through the rings to enable the fabric to be pulled up.

(c) Festoon blinds (sometimes called Austrian blinds). These are becoming increasingly popular and are a decorative way of disguising an ugly window or an unattractive view. These blinds too are attached to a batten at the top of the window and are drawn up by cords and rings attached to the back of the blind. They are, however, permanently gathered both across the width and down the length of the blind and hang in 'festoons' across the windows. They are very feminine and perhaps best used in bedrooms and bathrooms. Thin, lightweight fabrics make for the best effect, but linings can be used.

(d) 'Pulling-up curtains' are similar to festoon blinds, with cords and rings, but they hang flat when the cords are released. This is because they have no vertical gathering and therefore take less fabric than festoon blinds. Not all patterned fabrics work well with these curtains, so choose small designs or random match patterns for a pleasing effect. They are best lined.

2
Tracks, Fittings and Accessories

So many different tracks, rods, decorative poles and fittings are available that it is sometimes very difficult to know which to choose. They have been developed and improved over the last few years and a very wide selection now exists, for all possible needs. Several of the manufacturers produce useful booklets to help with the choice of tracks and accessories and these are well worth studying before a choice is made. Most large soft-furnishing departments have good displays of curtain hardware, and it is advisable to compare their differences and to understand their various functions.

For best results, the points made on the following pages should be considered before a selection is made.

Tracks and Poles

(1) Well-made tracks and fittings are essential for the smooth running of curtains, and it is wise to examine them carefully before purchase. Some tracks and poles are easier to fix than others, and some have combined hooks and runners. Some have cording systems built in, so that the curtains do not get soiled by constant handling. Other poles and tracks have no cording facilities, and therefore no overlap fixture at the centre. Most poles have decorative finials at the ends, which vary in style. Plastic and aluminium tracks can be either very decorative, or unobtrusive; their choice depends on the effect required. Some tracks are flexible, and bend easily to negotiate curves and corners.

(2) Not all tracks are equally pleasing to the eye but some can be covered successfully with curtain fabric or wallpaper, which itself can give a pleasing effect in some situations.

(3) Many plastic tracks are not strong enough to take the weight of heavy or interlined curtains, so care must be taken to choose a track or pole strong enough to carry the weight of the curtains they are to support.

(4) Decide on the style of curtains that best suits the architectural period of the room.

(5) Select the type of fabric and the style of curtain that enhances the decorative scheme of the room and takes into account its aspect. This governs the quality and type of track or pole, since it may have to support the weight of heavy interlined curtains or, alternatively, may only have to support small curtains needing only lightweight tracks.

(6) Decide whether a wooden, brass, or pewter finish is appropriate to the decor of the room, or whether a plastic or aluminium finish is preferable. Poles can be reeded or plain and are decorative features in themselves. Some of the simple, inexpensive wooden poles (even broom handles!) can be successfully covered with fabric to create an original design or they can be painted or varnished to suit the scheme. Most poles are packed complete with all necessary rings, brackets, screws and finials, but extra rings and brackets can be purchased separately if required. Some poles are extendible, to give the length required, but some are not. Most poles are for straight runs only, which means that they cannot be used round bowed windows (*fig. 13*).

(7) If a plastic or aluminium track is chosen, select one to suit the style of window treatment. Make sure that it is either decoratively suitable, or as unobtrusive as possible in use. If necessary, make sure that it can be easily covered with

wallpaper or fabric, for some tracks, by the very nature of their design, are not suitable for this treatment; the glide hooks or runners would not run smoothly if the track was covered in this way.

(8) If nets and sheers are in question, use the special inexpensive rods or lightweight tracks available. These can be purchased for either ceiling or wall fixing, and are obtainable with or without a cording set. More complicated tracks are available, with double fittings, enabling nets and sheers to be hung on an inner track, with the main curtains on an outer track. Alternatively, choose tension rods that support net curtains neatly without brackets. They spring out to grip the inside of the frame.

(9) When treating a door, make sure that the track or pole will accommodate the curtains off the frame, so that the door can move freely. Or, alternatively, use a swinging rod that swings the curtain open and away from the door. For glazed and half-glazed doors special door rods can be fixed to the top and bottom of the door so that the curtain hangs close to the glass.

(10) If a pelmet or valance is being used the track will not show, so its purpose is purely functional. Remember, however, to choose one that is strong enough to support the curtains chosen. Some manufacturers offer curtain tracks and valance rails combined in one fitting, but this is only suitable for use with a valance. It is not suitable where a pelmet is to be used.

(11) When making curtains for use around a curved window or into an awkward corner, use a flexible track which will bend easily. Not all tracks are meant to bend, and some are suitable for straight runs only. Bending some tracks could mean that the runners would not run smoothly.

(12) Before using a new track spray it lightly with a silicone wax polish — this will help the runners to glide smoothly.

Fittings

Figs 13–15 show some of the tracks and poles that are available, together with other fittings and accessories such as overlap arms and hooks and runners.

Runners

Having chosen the track or pole, you will find there are usually special gliders or runners that fit on to a particular track. Rings are available for poles in various sizes, and finishes vary from natural wood to brass. Some decorative poles have D-shaped ring slides so that a cording system can be incorporated.

Runners for plastic and aluminium tracks vary between ones that hang from a smooth track to ones that slot into a groove at the back of a plain track. Some runners are designed to take many different types of curtain headings as well as curtains with detachable linings.

Fig. 13 *Curtain poles of different designs*

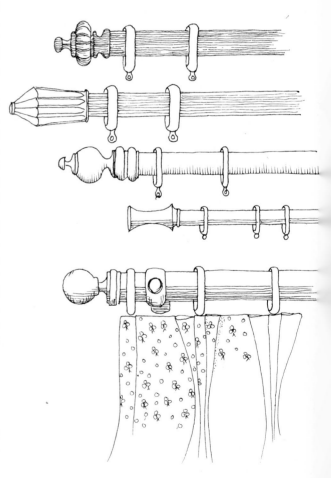

22

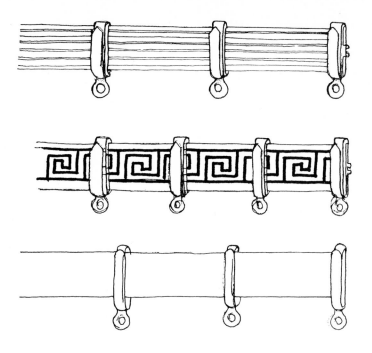

Fig. 14 *Tracks vary in design and weight*

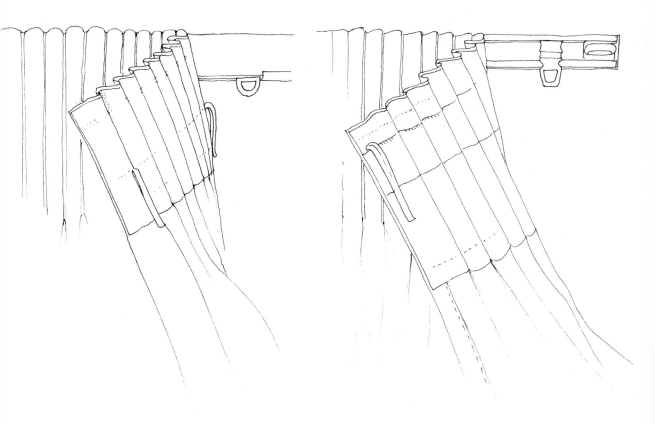

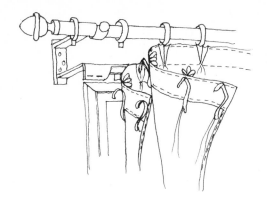

Fig. 15 *Double rod bracket for two sets of curtains*

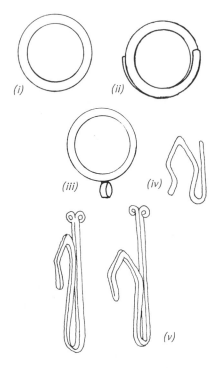

Fig. 16 *Curtain rings and hooks (i) Sew-on rings for café curtains (ii) Split rings for festoon and Roman blinds (iii) Café rings for use with hooks (iv) Stab-in pin hooks for use with hand-made headings (v) Slip-in hooks for use with commercial heading tapes*

Hooks

Hooks are used to enable the curtain to be hung from the runners or rings on the track or pole. Hooks are inserted into the curtain tape or heading at the back of the curtains, and then into the runners or holes in the curtain rings (*fig. 16*). They are made of plastic or metal, and vary in size and design according to the type of heading tape used. Some heading tapes require special hooks: for example, some of the pleated headings make use of special long hooks which stiffen the heading as well as forming a pleat or pleats at the top of the curtain. Simple hooks can be used with many of the commercial tapes, but this should be checked when the heading tape is purchased. Hooks are normally inserted into the heading tape at approximately 10 cm (4 in) intervals.

With a hand-made heading it is possible, nowadays, to use special stab-in pin hooks instead of those needing to be sewn in at the back of the heading. This makes hand-made headings less time-consuming to construct and easier to handle.

Accessories

Constant handling of curtains can soil them quickly. One way of avoiding this is to use a cording set, which can be incorporated in one of the many tracks available. If a cording set is not used, consider buying curtain pull rods or draw rods, which are designed for the same purpose (*fig. 17*). These are attached to the leading glider in the centre of the window and are hidden behind the leading edge of the curtain.

Weights can be used in nets and sheer curtains to improve their draping qualities. It is not usually necessary to use special weights when making up medium to heavyweight curtains, but they do sometimes improve the draping qualities of lightweight curtains, sheers and nets. Special leadweight tape is, however, available and can be purchased by the metre to suit all weights of fabric (*fig. 18*). Alternatively, small lead weights can be purchased in different sizes. These should be covered with a square of fabric and then stitched into the mitre at each corner of the curtain.

Velcro

Velcro is a 'touch and close' fastening made in the form of two tapes and surfaces. One surface is covered with tiny nylon hooks which catch onto the fuzz of the other when the two surfaces are pressed together. To open, simply pull the surfaces apart. A strip of each tape is sewn or stuck onto each surface; this can be used successfully when making pelmets or valances, or where the fabric needs to be fixed to wood.

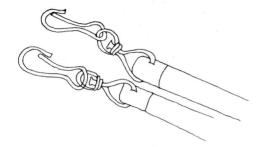

Fig. 17 *Using draw rods and pull cords avoids soiling curtains*

Fig. 18 *Leadweight tape used in curtains improves their draping qualities*

3
Colour, Design and Fabrics

Colour

There is no doubt that colour and the way we use it has a great influence on our lives. Our mood is reflected in the colours that we wear, and our personalities are reflected in the colours we use in the home.

Colours themselves do not change, but fashion suggests a different emphasis year by year. This is noticeable in the clothes that we wear and the way we put them together. We can change our clothes more frequently than most of us can change our furnishings, so it is important that we try to understand how to use colour to the best possible effect. In this way we shall be happy and confident with the furnishings we choose — for they are not easily discarded.

To understand colour is to know something of how it works. Colour is only present when there is light. This is passed through a prism and is broken up into a spectrum which is visible to the human eye. The three components in this spectrum (from which all other colours originate) are red, blue and yellow. These are called the primary colours. Secondary colours are produced by the mixing of the two adjoining primary colours. Orange (made by mixing red and yellow), green (by mixing blue and yellow) and purple (by mixing blue and red). Thus, the colour wheel is formed. Hundreds of different colour tones can be obtained by mixing secondary colours together in varying amounts and darkening them or lightening them with black or white.

Black and white are the extremes of the 'neutrals', which can also be greys and off-whites. These neutrals do not count as colours, as they have no colour in themselves. Black absorbs light and sharpens or intensifies the colours around it, so making ceilings look lower and rooms appear smaller. White reflects light and absorbs other colours around it, so making rooms look larger and ceilings higher. The neutrals of black and white, and their varying tones of greys and off-whites, are often used as a background to the primary or secondary colours. These are excellent for background items that cannot be changed too often, since many colours and tones work well with them.

Colour is very much influenced by its surroundings and can take on an entirely fresh tone when accompanied by different colour hues or textures. The intensity of light also influences colour because of the amount of light that is reflected; for example, candlelight and sunlight will produce quite different effects when focused on the same object. When choosing colours for fabrics, therefore, look at them both in daylight and artifical light to check the effects they produce.

Colour sets the mood of a room; colours can be cool, warm or neutral. The cool colours of the colour spectrum are greens, blues and purples. These are best used in rooms that are warm and face south and west. Cool colours used in north and east-facing rooms, or ones that feel cold, would create an unwelcoming effect. On the other hand they can successfully cool down a sunny, warm room facing south. The warm colours of the colour spectrum are reds, oranges and yellow; they are good used in north and east-facing rooms because they create a warm and comfortable mood.

To use colour effectively it is important to know which colours work well together and how to create a good balance of those colours. Do not use too many colours together, or the result will be an untidy, cluttered look. Rather, use two or three colours, letting one of these dominate so as to strike a good overall balance. Use small amounts of one colour to give impact and emphasis to accessories. When planning a colour scheme bear in the mind the following guidelines.

A monochromatic scheme is one using a single colour only, but in varying proportions of tone. Interest can be given to this one colour by using various textures in the window, floor and wall coverings, which will all be related together because of their one common colour. When choosing such a scheme use small amounts of accent colours that contrast well with the colour chosen. Contrast colours are those that lie opposite to one another on the colour wheel.

Related colour schemes make use of two or three colours that adjoin each other on the colour spectrum. These are called harmonious colours. Use of them creates a restful scheme because the colours are 'in harmony' with each other and therefore work well together (e.g. yellow/orange, yellow/green).

Complementary colour schemes use two colours that are opposite to one another in the colour wheel. As these colours are in contrast with each other they produce dramatic schemes and often need the help of the neutrals to offset the drama and to provide a quiet background.

Discordant schemes are produced when colours are used out of their natural order in the colour wheel. They are neither in harmony, nor complementary to each other and so do not co-exist well. This makes them difficult to use together successfully and creates an inharmonious effect that offends the eye.

Experiment with colour schemes before making a final choice by collecting swatches of fabrics and samples of wallpapers and paints. Try them together in the room where they are to be used. If possible, buy a length of the fabric or a roll of the wallpaper to make sure that it really satisfies the eye. Make sure that the colour balance you plan to use works well and follows the guidelines given above.

Texture is another dimension of the decorating scheme. It adds interest to a room without the need for colour and can be used profusely in a monochromatic scheme where the emphasis is on one colour only. Texture affects the value of colour, since rough textures absorb light but shiny ones reflect it. Variations in texture give interest to a room, so experiment by collecting as many fabrics as possible in the same colour, but with different textures.

Design

The design, or pattern, of fabrics plays an important part in a room's colour scheme. When using a patterned fabric choose this before the plain or textured fabrics that are to go with it. It is more difficult to find an appealing print or pattern than it is to find a plain or textured fabric that matches or contrasts. So choose the pattern first.

Too much pattern in a room can produce a cluttered effect, though the tendency now is to use two, or even three-colour co-ordinated prints. This works well if the prints are carefully co-ordinated, so make sure that the fabrics used share the same common colours. This is made easier now by the many ranges of co-ordinating fabrics available. They have been professionally designed to take into account balance and contrast.

Use small or geometric prints in small rooms or at small windows, keeping larger designs for large windows or rooms. It is important to scale the size of the print or pattern to the window or room where it is to be used. A large pattern at a small window will focus too much attention, dominating the scheme and giving a lack of balance to the overall picture.

Try out fabrics by obtaining swatches and living with them for a time. It is sometimes necessary to buy a small quantity of each fabric to make sure that they work well in the proportion in which they are to be used. This is well worth while, and money well spent.

Take time when choosing fabrics and creating a colour scheme. Do not be rushed into buying something you are not sure about, and have not considered carefully. Never buy fabric in sales unless you have first had time to consider it, and know that it is exactly what you want. Never be tempted to buy without the other swatches and samples in your hand — it is almost impossible to carry colour in the eye.

Make a point of looking at good design, and notice how pattern and shape is used. Much can be learned by studying the work of professional designers in different fields (e.g. television, films, window displays, etc.) and being constantly aware of the 'design' that surrounds us. Visits to historic houses and stately homes can be sources of inspiration for design and colour.

When designing the decor for a house or flat,

try to achieve a feeling of spaciousness and continuity. This is best done by relating the rooms together by the use of colour. One colour common to all rooms can be used in different amounts and proportions. Make a separate scheme for each room or area using varying amounts of colour, texture and pattern in each. For example, in one room a colour can dominate, but in another it can act as a contrast or a background for a different scheme; or use it simply as an accent colour. In this way there will be continuity in the finished scheme and a pleasing result will be achieved. Colours can also be linked together successfully by the choice of a basic floor covering in a neutral tone. This makes a harmonious background for many decorative schemes.

Fabrics

Care must be taken when selecting fabric for curtains and blinds to make sure that it suits both the decorative scheme and the purpose for which it is needed. Consider also the position of the curtains or blinds — whether they will be in a rural setting or in an urban location where they will need more frequent washing or cleaning. Curtains and blinds in kitchens get dirty quickly, so it is advisable to choose a fabric that washes well or one that can be sponged over quite easily. Children's rooms and playrooms usually need hard-wearing fabrics that wash or clean well; interlined curtains and insulated linings are useful in bedrooms where noise and light may be a problem. Textured fabrics attract the dust more easily than ones with a smooth surface and this may mean that they need cleaning more often.

When choosing fabrics for windows bear in mind the following points:

(1) Choose and buy the best quality fabric that you can afford — this may not necessarily be the most expensive, but it should be the one that offers the best value for money.

(2) When buying patterned fabric make sure that the pattern is printed correctly on the weft grain of the fabric if it is not woven into it. A fault of this kind can present many problems when making up, as each length of curtain or blind fabric should be cut to the weft grain to make it hang straight. However, if the pattern *is* badly printed, the fabric should be cut to the pattern to make it look aesthetically

correct. Cheap patterned fabrics are often badly printed and may not resist the light well.

(3) Make sure the fabric is fadeless, as it is often exposed to strong sunlight. If unlined curtains or blinds are being made, remember that they will not have the protection of a lining.

(4) Always ask to see the fabric draped, in order to check its draping qualities and to look at both pattern and colour. Patterns and colours look very different when lying flat on a counter. If possible, ask for a large pattern sample so that it can be considered in both daylight and artificial light in the setting for which it is intended. Some retailers are pleased to provide large pattern samples which are returnable when a choice has been made. It is worth asking if these are available.

(5) Generally, it is best to buy fabric that is recommended for curtains or blinds. Upholstery fabrics are usually too heavy to drape well, and may also crease badly because of their high linen content. Dress fabrics are not made to withstand constant exposure to light and atmosphere. However, some can be used successfully for curtains, but remember that they will not wear as long as furnishing fabrics; also they are narrower and will possibly involve more seams.

(6) Check whether the fabric needs dry cleaning or whether it is washable only, in which case it should be shrink resistant. If making a roller blind for a kitchen, make sure that the fabric can be sponged clean.

(7) When choosing patterned fabric remember that a larger quantity is needed in order to match the patterns correctly. Small pattern repeats or random match patterns are therefore more economical than large repeats, where much wastage can occur. An allowance of one pattern repeat to each length or 'drop' of curtain or blind should be made. Some patterns work better than others, depending on the treatment of the window and the number and size of the windows being dressed.

(8) Choose a heading to suit the fabric. Some fabrics look better when less fullness is used in the heading, showing up the pattern to advantage. Consider using either single or double pleats instead of triple pleats. These need much less fullness and therefore less fabric.

(9) Check that the fabric is free from flaws. These should have been marked with a coloured cotton on the selvedge and should be allowed for by the sales assistant.

(10) Buy enough fabric to complete the project. It is not always possible to obtain exact colour matches should extra fabric be needed later.

(11) Make a sketch of the window or doors being treated, showing accurate measurements. Keep it for reference whilst making up the curtains or blinds.

(12) Period curtains often had braids inset on the leading (side) edges to prevent the fabric from wearing. Sometimes borders were used, and sewn on separately. They could then be replaced when worn. Nowadays, braids, fringes, decorative and contrasting borders and frilled edges can be used very effectively for curtains and blinds, pelmets and valances. Borders are particularly useful when curtains need to be lengthened, and they should be added to the leading edges of the curtain as well as the lower edges. Curtain lining sateen in contrasting colours can be used effectively for this and is an economical choice of fabric.

There are many suitable fabrics available for curtains and blinds, ranging from the natural fibres of silk and cotton to the many man-made fibres which they emulate.

Natural fabrics are made from raw materials of animal and vegetable sources; man-made fabrics are those made from fibres manufactured by chemically treating raw materials such as minerals and vegetables.

Cotton

The cotton plant is a flowering shrub whose blooms become covered with tufts of cotton wool. This is carded and spun to produce thread and fabric. There is little wastage in the production of cotton as all the fibres can be used and it is one of the most versatile of the natural fibres.

Cotton is strong and hard-wearing, washes well and can be easily dyed and printed. It can be treated with several different easy-care finishes and can be rendered shrink-resistant, crease-resistant, stain-repellent, drip-dry, minimum-iron, flameproof and water-repellent. It can also be glazed, which makes an attractive finish and also makes the fabric dirt-

resistant. It can be treated with special insulating properties or to make a suitable fabric for lining curtains. It is often mixed with other yarns to produce both light and heavyweight fabrics.

Linen

Linen is a hard-wearing fabric produced from the fibres of the flax plant. It is very durable and does not shrink, but in its natural form creases easily. It is often blended with other fibres to give furnishing fabrics added strength.

Wool

Woollen thread is produced from the twisted strands of hair shorn from the bodies of sheep, the alpaca and some species of goat. The fibres of sheep's wool vary in length and thickness according to the breed. The finer fibres are made into furnishing fabrics and are often blended with other fibres to give a crease-resistant quality. Wool is soft, warm and resilient. Wool dyes well and can be rendered shrink-resistant, water-repellent, stain-repellent and mothproof.

Silk

Silk is the fine thread which is reeled from the cocoon of the silkworm larva, then wound on bobbins to be woven into fabric. Silk is expensive to produce as the insects which spin the fibres are costly to rear. It has great strength but is weakened by strong sunlight. Its use has now been largely replaced by that of man-made fibres such as rayon, as these, using vegetable cellulose, are much quicker and cheaper to produce. Silk is, therefore, a luxury fabric which is now rarely used for curtains and blinds.

Great progress has been made in the manufacture of man-made fibres and new techniques are being introduced to improve the properties of the fabrics. It is now possible to dye man-made fibres to create more subtle colours than those originally obtained, and it is often very difficult to distinguish them from the natural fibres which they imitate.

Man-made fibres are produced by chemically treating basic raw materials such as wood pulp, petroleum extracts, by-products of coal, casein, cotton linters and groundnuts. Most of the fabrics produced are not absorbent and tend to look dirty rather more quickly than fabrics made from natural fibres. This is because the dirt stays on the surface and is not absorbed by the fabric. But it makes them easy to clean. Most synthetic fibres can be blended with natural fibres or other man-made fibres to produce fabrics with varying uses and finishes, strengths and resilience. Most man-made fabrics wash and dry quickly, retaining their shape well. They do not shrink or stretch and usually have a good resistance to sunlight, which makes them an ideal choice for curtains and blinds. Sheers and nets made from man-made fibres such as nylon should never be allowed to get too dirty before washing.

Bump (see Glossary)

This is a thick, soft fluffy fabric made from cotton waste and is available bleached or unbleached. It is used for interlining curtains and pelmets and is a good insulator. It cannot be washed and must be dry cleaned only.

Buckram

This is obtainable by the meter and varies in width from 7.5—15 cm (3—6 in). It can be used for stiffening hand-made curtain headings, and can be ironed on to the fabric using a steam iron.

Cotton lace

This is available in wide widths specially for soft furnishings. It is mostly used for bedspreads but can make very effective curtains. However, it will shrink when washed, so generous allowances should be made for fullness and hems.

Domette (see Glossary)

This has the same uses as bump but is not quite so thick and fluffy. A raised interlining, similar to domette but made from viscose and nylon, is now available and this also needs to be dry cleaned and should not be washed.

Dupion

This is a most versatile soft-furnishing fabric with an attractive appearance of slubbed 'silk'. It is mostly made from man-made fibres, but is available in a very wide range of colours. It is very suitable for curtains as it drapes well and is moderately priced. It has a luxurious look when interlined. As it frays very badly the edges should be overcast as soon as the fabric has been cut. Always make generous seam and hem allowances.

Felt

This can be used successfully for curtains in certain situations. It is a non-fraying fabric available in wide widths in many colours.

Gingham

This is available in weights suitable for curtains and blinds and with its fresh crisp look is particularly suitable for kitchens, bathrooms and children's rooms.

Holland

This is the traditional firm fabric used for making roller blinds. Many colours and patterns are now available in wide widths.

Pillow ticking

This black-and-white striped fabric can make attractive hard-wearing blinds or curtains and is inexpensive to use.

Polyester/cotton sheeting

This sheeting fabric which is made partly from natural cotton fibres and partly from man-made fibres comes in wide widths and is suitable also for making curtains and blinds. It washes well, needs little ironing and is made in co-ordinating plain colours and prints.

PVC (Polyvinyl chloride)

This is strong, has a shiny surface and is resistant to chemicals. It can be easily wiped clean and is useful when making roller blinds for kitchens and bathrooms. When working with PVC do not pin or tack the fabric as this would damage it. Hold fabric in place, when necessary, with sellotape or paper clips. Machine using a long stitch and a needle suitable for medium to heavyweight fabrics. If the fabric is very shiny and does not slide properly beneath the presser foot, use tissue paper underneath the fabric to prevent it from sticking. Alternatively, spread a little talcum powder on the shiny side of the fabric to lubricate it through the machine, or use a special presser foot with sliding rolls. Make sure that the stitching is right first time because unpicking will result in holes in the fabric.

Pelmet buckram

Pelmet buckram is golden brown in colour and is made from coarse canvas impregnated with glue. It is sold by the meter in narrow widths of 45.5 cm (18 in) wide and is used for making curtain tie-backs as well as pelmets.

Rep
Reps are reversible fabrics with transverse ribs. The lighter, more loosely woven ones are suitable for curtains and blinds as they drape better than the heavier qualities, which are more suited to upholstery.

Sateen
This is a closely woven cotton fabric normally used for lining curtains and blinds. It is available in a wide range of colours.

Tweed
This was originally produced from Cheviot sheeps' wool in a village on the river Tweed in the UK. Nowadays, however, 'tweeds' are readily available in both natural and man-made fabrics in a variety of textures and weaves. Some loosely woven acrylic fabrics in this category stretch a little with the weight of the curtain when made up. In this case the curtains should be hung for a while before the hem is finally stitched.

Velvet
Velvet and velveteen can be made from silk, cotton and synthetics and vary in quality with the fibres used, the closeness of the pile and the background onto which the pile is woven. When making curtains take care that the pile is placed in the same direction in each curtain — this is usually downwards in soft furnishings, upwards in upholstery. This avoids dust being caught in the pile and also gives a pleasing effect when the curtains are draped. It is necessary to pin and tack velvets carefully before machining seams, for when the piles are placed on top of one another the fabric tends to slip out of position.

4
Tools and Equipment

Always ensure that tools and equipment are in good working order, keeping them together so that they are instantly available when needed. Replenish the workbox regularly with new pins and needles and look after them carefully. Bent needles result in poor workmanship and rusty pins will mark fabrics.

Buy the best quality tools you can afford and only use them for the purpose for which they were intended. When scissors need sharpening it is best to return them to the manufacturer or have them professionally ground.

Pins
Choose steel dressmaking pins as these will not pin-mark fabrics. Glass-headed pins are made from broken needles and are very sharp, so extra care is needed when using them. Never use rusty pins. Invest in a new packet from time to time and keep them carefully in the box or tin provided for the purpose. Do not leave pins in fabric longer than necessary as they will mark the fabric if left in for long periods. If a finger is pricked and blood accidentally stains the fabric, remove it by chewing a piece of tacking thread and rubbing it onto the bloodstain. This will remove the stain without leaving a water mark.

Needles
Make sure the needle is sharp and free from rust. A selection of needles of various types for different fabrics produces good results. Use Sharps and Betweens 7–9 for general use.

Threads
It is important to use the correct thread. Try to match the thread colour to the fabric, but have it one tone darker. Use synthetic threads with synthetic fabrics. These are strong and can damage natural fibres, but cotton thread used on synthetic fabric would shrink more than the synthetic fabric and cause it to pucker. For general use and for medium-weight fabrics of linen, cotton, etc., choose medium-weight threads. Use stronger thread for heavier materials, silk or fine gauge cotton for finer fabrics, and tacking cotton for basting.

Scissors
A sharp pair of cutting-out shears with specially bent handles makes the cutting out of fabric for curtains and blinds easier. A smaller pair of scissors, 12.5–14 cm (5–5½ in), is useful for cutting threads, etc. Choose the best quality possible.

Measure
A wooden yardstick is an invaluable aid for measuring curtains accurately. An inexpensive one can be obtained from most wallpaper shops. Alternatively, use a metal rule. A large set square is also useful when making roller blinds, to ensure that the fabric is cut correctly. Always use a rigid rule when measuring curtains, blinds and windows.

Tape measure
Choose a fibre-glass or linen tape with a stiffened end. These are the most reliable as they will not stretch easily.

Tailor's chalk
This is extremely useful for marking fabric when cutting out curtains and blinds, and for making pleats in hand-made headings. It is obtainable in several colours as well as white (which is easy to remove).

Seam ripper
This is a small ripping tool used for unpicking seams and stitches quickly.

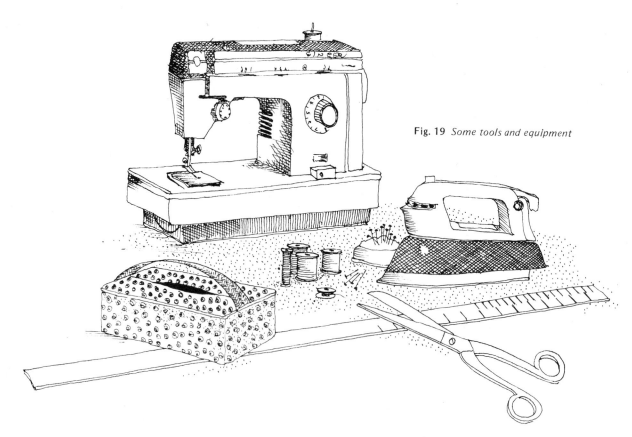

Fig. 19 *Some tools and equipment*

Ironing board and iron

A wide board is the most useful and a steam or heavy iron the most suitable when making curtains and blinds. Man-made fibres sometimes leave marks on the base of the iron, so make sure the base is cleaned regularly. Always have the iron readily available for pressing seams as the work progresses.

Cutting out surface

If possible use a large dining room or kitchen table. If this is not available a wallpaper pasting table provides an ideal surface and can also be used for pressing if covered with several thicknesses of blanket. This type of table is a good investment as it can be folded up and stored easily and it is relatively inexpensive. Do not be tempted to make curtains on the floor; this is not satisfactory and can be extremely tiring to the back.

Weight

A weight is very useful when making curtains and blinds. It is used to prevent the fabric from slipping from the table, and a simple one can be made easily from a brick or an old iron. Cover the brick or iron with pieces of old blanket or wadding and then cover with some strong fabric, making a handle in fabric or upholstery webbing so that the weight is easy to move. Its padded top can be used as a pin cushion.

Thimble

Choose a metal one, to protect the middle finger. Thimbles are particularly important when sewing firm fabric such as roller blind fabric and coarse materials.

Sewing machine

A sewing machine is useful when making curtains and blinds as long seams often have to be worked, and where heading tapes are used on curtains, they are best machine-stitched into position. An electrically operated machine is an ideal choice as both hands can then be used to control the work which is often heavy because of the bulk of the fabric.

A sewing machine should last a lifetime, so time and careful thought should be given to its selection. If possible choose a lightweight, versatile machine with a free arm, and one capable of producing zig-zag as well as straight stitching. When choosing a machine with soft furnishings in mind make sure that it is strong enough to take several thicknesses of fabric. Also important is the provision of zig-zag stitching and a free arm; these are probably more important than the facility to sew a wide range of embroidery stitches which may be used rather infrequently.

Having bought a machine make sure that you know how it operates. Take advantage of any post sales tuition that may be offered and practise using the attachments. Learn to thread up the machine quickly and accurately and to change the needles and feet to suit the fabric and thread being used. It pays to study the instruction booklets carefully.

Look after the machine. Clean and oil it regularly and have it professionally serviced from time to time. Keep the machine covered when not in use and do not keep it in a cold, damp room or in direct heat. Never leave it with the electric plug connected, as this could burn out the motor.

A festoon blind trimmed with a contrasting plain fabric.

5
Seams and Stitches

These are some of the seams and stitches used when making curtains and blinds.

Seams

Plain seam

This is the most usual seam employed when making lined curtains and blinds, and can be worked easily by machine. Place the fabric with the raw edges together, right sides facing and tack 1.3 cm (½ in) from the edge. Stitch the seam, remove the tacking stitches and press open. When making lined curtains or blinds it is not usually necessary to neaten the raw edges, but if the fabric frays badly these can be finished with a row of zig-zag stitching or overcast by hand (*fig. 20*).

When machining a curtain or blind seam, stitch down the length of the seam from the top to the bottom. Make sure that the nap (pile) runs in the same direction on each side of the seam — a point to watch

particularly when sewing velvet or corduroy. When machining PVC use strips of tissue paper between the fabric and the machine presser foot to make stitching easier. Do not tack or use pins on PVC as this will spoil the fabric. Instead, use sticky tape to hold the fabrics together whilst stitching.

Fig. 21 *French seam, showing raw edges enclosed*

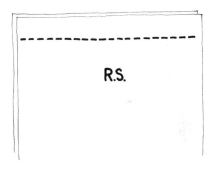

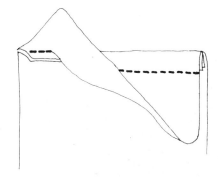

Fig. 20 *Neatening a plain seam with a zig-zag or an overcasting stitch*

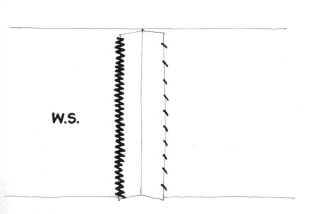

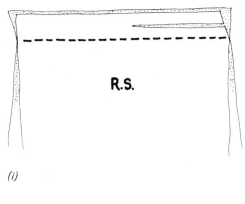

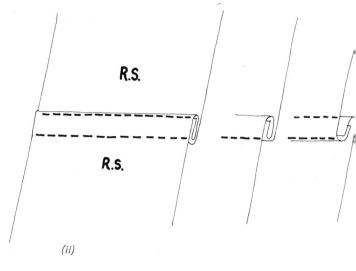

(i)

Fig. 22 *(i) Seam allowance trimmed to make a flat fell seam (ii) Finished flat fell seam*

(ii)

French seam

This seam is often used when widths of very lightweight curtain or blind fabric are being joined together. It is only suitable for fabrics that are not thick and bulky. Place the two pieces of fabric together wrong sides facing and stitch approximately 6 mm–1.3 cm (¼–½ in) in from the edge, depending on whether the fabric frays easily or not. Trim this seam and turn to the wrong side. With right sides together, tack and machine to enclose the raw edges (*fig. 21*).

Flat fell seam

This is a useful seam when joining widths of fabric for unlined curtains or blinds or where a strong enclosed seam is required. It is hard-wearing, but the stitching shows on the right side of the fabric. Place the wrong sides of the fabric together and have the raw edges even. Tack and machine 1.3 cm (½ in) in from the edge. Press seam open. Trim one side of the seam to 6 mm (¼ in) and turn in the raw edge of the other side 3 mm ($\frac{1}{8}$ in). Fold this over the trimmed edge and machine close to the fold, or slipstitch by hand (*fig. 22*).

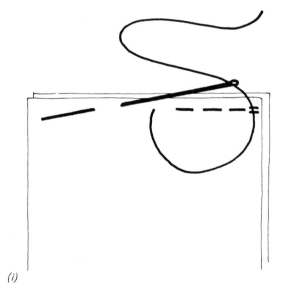

(i)

Stitches

Tacking (basting)

Tacking, or basting, is temporary stitching used to hold two or more thicknesses of fabric together.

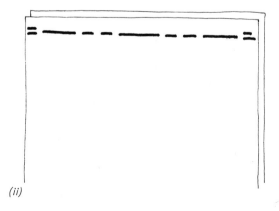

Fig. 23 *Tacking stitches (i) Tacking using long, equal stitches (ii) Tacking using one long and two short stitches*

(ii)

38

Stitch from right to left. There are two types of basting: (a) long equal stitches of about 1.3 cm (½ in) with equal space between and (b) two stitches of 1.3 cm (½ in) and one stitch 2.5 cm (1 in) long. The latter is particularly useful when tacking up curtains as it is quick to work. Start and finish both types of basting with a backstitch (*fig. 23*).

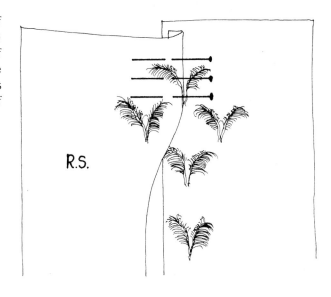

R.S.

Fig. 24 *Neatening a raw edge with overcasting*

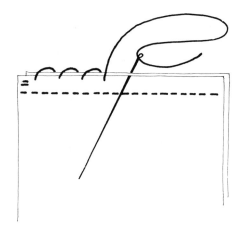

Fig. 25 *Slipstitching*

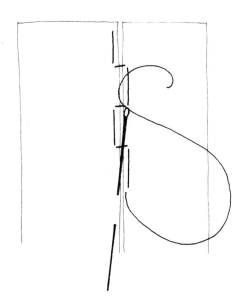

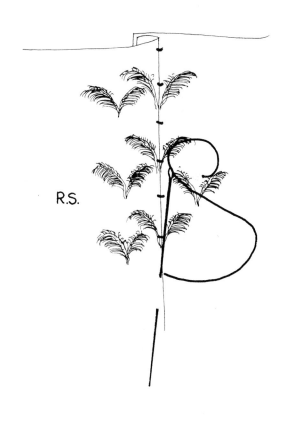

R.S.

Fig. 26 *Slip tacking (outside tacking)*

39

Overcasting

This is used to neaten a raw edge to prevent fraying. Work from left to right, bringing the needle through at an acute angle and taking the thread over the raw edge (*fig. 24*).

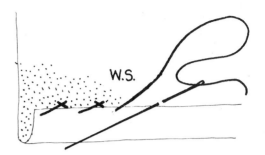

Slipstitching

This is for joining folded edges together invisibly, as on a mitred corner of a curtain. Pick up a thread from one fold and slide the needle through the fold for 6 mm (¼ in), and then put the needle into the other fold and carefully draw up the thread. Do not pull tightly or puckering could occur (*fig. 25*).

Slip tacking (outside tacking)

This is particularly useful when matching patterns on widths of curtain or blind fabric when accuracy in matching is vital. It is worked on the right side of the fabric so that the pattern is easily visible. Fold in the edge of one piece of fabric on to its wrong side and place onto the right side of the piece of fabric to be matched. Place the pins into position horizontally, carefully matching the pattern. Slip-tack, taking a stitch on the fold of the one side and slipping the needle down through the fold on the other. Stitch the seam in the exact position of the tacking line so that the pattern matches accurately (*fig. 26*).

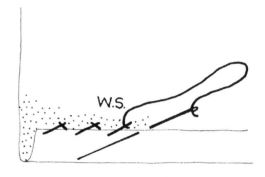

Fig. 27 *Herringbone stitch used to secure interlining to a curtain*

Fig. 28 *Serge stitching*

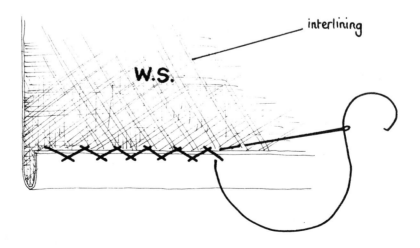

Herringbone stitch

This is used for making hems on heavier curtain fabrics where extra strength is necessary, and for securing interlining to the curtain fabric when making interlined curtains. The stitch is worked from left to right, usually over a raw edge. Keep the needle pointing to the left and the thread on the right hand side of the stitching. Pick up a thread of curtain fabric and a thread of interlining alternately, keeping the stitches as near as possible to the fold (*fig. 27*).

Serging

This is used when turning down a single-fold hem round the raw edges of a curtain or blind before the lining is applied. Sew from left to right picking up a thread from the single thickness of fabric and then inserting the needle into the folded hem. The two stitches should be made in one movement and should be approximately 1.3 cm (½ in) in length. The stitches should not show on the right side of the fabric (*fig. 28*).

Locking

This is a long, loose stitch approximately 10–15 cm (4–6 in) in length, used to lock or secure the lining or interlining to the curtain fabric so that they do not come apart. It is worked from left to right down the length of the curtain. The stitches should not show on either the right side of the curtain or the lining and they must be kept very loose so that no pulling occurs when the curtains are hanging (*fig. 29*). Try to use one long length of thread when working this stitch.

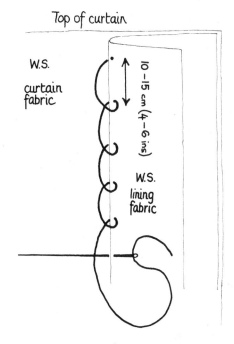

Top of curtain

W.S.

curtain fabric

10–15 cm (4–6 ins)

W.S. lining fabric

Fig. 29 *Lock stitch*

A festoon blind trimmed with rosettes at the head.

6
Linings and Interlinings

Most curtains and some blinds are enhanced by a lining. Although nets and some sheer fabrics do not need lining, most fabrics drape better when lined. This also protects the fabric against strong sunlight, dust, dirt and frost. All of these damage the fibres of the fabric and make it wear out more quickly. Some curtain fabrics last for many years when well protected, sometimes outliving their linings. In this case it is worth relining the curtains to give them a fresh lease of life.

The choice of fabric used for the curtains or blinds often determines whether or not a lining is needed. For example, unlined curtains are probably more practical in kitchens and bathrooms because they are easy to launder but where good insulation is required a lining and/or an interlining would be a better choice.

Choose a good quality cotton sateen for lining and make sure it is the best one available. Poor-quality lining fabrics are a false economy as they wear out more quickly and often shrink badly when cleaned or washed. Lining sateen is available in various widths and colours as well as in natural and white. This makes it easy to have all the curtains looking uniform from the outside of the house, which gives a more pleasing effect than having different colours at each window.

Also available is a metal insulated lining fabric which makes the curtain completely draughtproof. It is therefore a good choice when preparing curtains for doors or draughty windows where an interlining would be inappropriate.

Cotton sateen is light in weight, and because it is not evenly woven it is not possible to pull a thread to straighten the edge. Each length should be cut either against a square table or cut using a set square. Do not try to tear it.

Detachable linings can be made for curtains, using a special curtain lining tape. These linings are easily removed for washing and can be changed from one pair of curtains to another. The lining is made separately from the curtains and has its own tape. It is attached to the curtain by the same hooks which suspend the curtain from the track. These linings do not have the same professional finish as permanently lined curtains and they do not hang or drape so well, but they are useful when curtains need to be washed frequently or when summer and winter curtains are used.

If economy is of prime importance curtains can be made entirely of lining sateen. There is a good range of colours and the effect is similar to a glazed chintz. Interest could be added with the application of a contrasting border of a patterned fabric or some other decorative trimming.

Interlined curtains have all the advantages of lined curtains and more. As well as helping the curtains to drape well, the interlining causes the texture or pattern of the fabric to be shown to the best advantage. It is particularly effective when more delicate furnishing fabrics are being used such as satin, dupion or silk, as the interlining gives the fabric 'body'. It is a very good insulator, keeping out both cold and noise. It is placed between the curtain fabric and the lining and is 'locked' into position.

Bump and domette (see *Glossary*) are the fabrics generally used for interlining curtains, but flanelette sheeting is also suitable. Bump is a thick, soft, fluffy fabric made from cotton waste and is available bleached or unbleached. Domette is similar in appearance but not quite so thick and fluffy. Neither one is washable, so interlined curtains must be dry cleaned. A raised interlining, similar to domette but made from viscose and nylon, is now available and this also needs to be dry cleaned and should not be washed.

It is certainly worth practising the technique of interlining curtains, as the finished result is well worth the extra time and expense involved. These curtains are extremely costly if made professionally.

A roller blind with a hand-painted design.

7

Curtains

Estimating Requirements and Cutting out the Fabric

When the curtain tracks or decorative rods have been chosen and fixed into position it is then possible to estimate the amount of fabric, lining and/or inter-lining required. The track or rod is usually placed 5–10 cm (2–4 in) above the window frame and should be extended 15–45.5 cm (6–18 in) at each side of the frame depending on the width of the window and the thickness of the curtain fabric. A wide window will need more room at each side to accommodate the curtains when drawn back. Heavily interlinined curtains also take up more space at either side of a window.

Measure the window carefully and decide on the exact position of the track or pole. A pole is a decorative feature and the curtains should hang below it. Use a wooden yardstick or rigid rule, as accurate measurements cannot be obtained with a tape measure. Draw a diagram and mark in all the appropriate measurements.

Decide where the curtains are to finish. There are three different lengths to choose from: (a) On the sill (b) Below the sill (c) Floor length (shown as A, B and C respectively in *fig. 30*). If the curtains are to hang to the sill they should finish 1.3 cm (½ in) above the sill; if they are to hang below the sill they should finish 5–10 cm (2–6 in) below the sill. If they are to be floor length they should finish within 1.3 cm (½ in) of the floor covering. This is called the 'finished' length. Avoid any in-between measurement as the curtains will be out of proportion to the window. It is a common mistake to make the curtains hang too far below the sill, which spoils the finished effect.

Two measurements are necessary to estimate the amount of fabric needed.

(1) The width of the track (not the window), measured from end to end.

(2) The finished length of the curtains, i.e. the 'drop', measured from the position from which the curtains will hang to the required bottom edge. To these measurements must be added an allowance for turnings of hems and headings. Allow 15–23 cm (6–9 in) inclusive.

When using patterned fabric allow an extra pattern repeat on each 'drop' of curtain when cutting. The 'drop' is the finished length of the curtain plus turnings. All the curtains should finish at the same

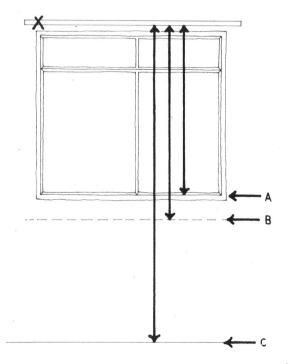

Fig. 30 *Deciding on the length of the curtains (A) On the sill (B) Below the sill (C) Floor length (X) Position of track*

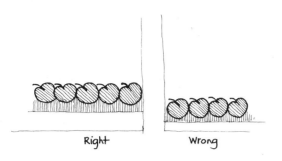

Right Wrong

Fig. 31 *Planning the curtains so that the pattern starts at the lower hem*

position on the pattern. Plan them so that the pattern starts at their lower edge after making an allowance for the hem (*fig. 31*). Half patterns are best put at the head of the curtains where gathers or pleats will make them less obvious.

Decide how many widths of fabric will be required to give the necessary fullness to the curtains. This depends on the weight and thickness of the fabric chosen and the heading selected. Remember that light unlined curtains need more fullness than heavy interlined ones. Here is a useful guide:

(1) Simple gathered headings on mediumweight fabrics require approximately one and a half times the width of the track.
(2) Pinch pleats on light/mediumweight fabrics require from two to two and a half times the width of the track.
(3) Pencil pleats and many of the other commercial heading tapes as well as sheers and net curtains require from two and a half to three times the width of the track.
(4) If the curtain track overlaps in the centre, allow 7.5–10 cm (3–4 in) extra on each curtain.
(5) For heavy fabrics and interlined curtains with a simple gathered heading allow one and a quarter to one and a half times the width of the track.

To obtain the required fullness it is often necessary to join widths and half widths together. Any half widths that have to be used should be joined so that they will hang at the outer sides of the window.

Always err on the generous side when estimating the amount of fullness needed - nothing looks worse than curtains that are skimped. It is preferable to

choose a less expensive fabric and use more, than to choose an expensive with too little fullness.

The same amount of fabric will be needed for the lining and interlining (if one is used) as for the curtains.

Whether making unlined, lined or interlined curtains or when making blinds, the rules for cutting out the fabric are the same.

(1) Place the material on a large square or rectangular table with the selvedge of the fabric running down the longest side. The end of the table can then be used to square up the fabric if necessary.
(2) If possible, draw a thread in order to get a straight line for cutting. It is not possible to draw a thread on some fabrics; in this case the fabric should be squared up with the table or a large set square to get an accurate cutting line which is at right angles to the selvedge.
(3) Cut plain fabric to the grain of the material. If a pattern is badly printed and is not on the grain, cut to the pattern so that the curtain when made will satisfy the eye.
(4) Cut out each length of curtain taking care to match patterns. Before cutting, measure and mark with pins or tailor's chalk. Use tailor's chalk and a meter stick to draw a straight

Fig. 32 *Snipping the selvedge threads to prevent the seams puckering*

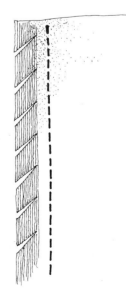

46

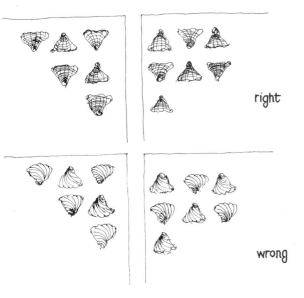

line on the position of the cut. Remember to allow for pattern repeats and turnings, and check these carefully before cutting.

(5) Mark the top of each length of curtain fabric as it is cut off the roll. This is important when using velvet or velour as the pile on the velvet should run down the curtain length so that dust can be easily removed from the fabric.

(6) Cut off all selvedges, for these often make the seams pucker. If the fabric frays badly snip the selvedge threads every 5 cm (2 in) instead, after the seam has been worked, to prevent it from puckering (*fig. 32*). Some sheer fabrics have a self-neatening type of weave at the selvedge and in this case it is not necessary to slash the selvedge or even make a hem to finish the edge.

(7) When using a patterned fabric cut off any wastage as the lengths are cut. If this is not done, confusion can arise when making up the curtains and matching the pattern repeats.

(8) Take care when matching and joining patterns. Pin and tack on the outside of the fabric to obtain an accurate match and make sure that the patterns match correctly (*figs 33 and 34*).

Figs 33 and 34 *Matching patterns for curtains and blinds*

Fig. 35 *Joining a bordered fabric means cutting away one of the borders*

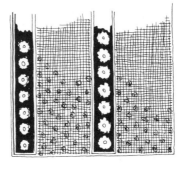

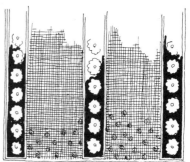

(9) When joining a width of fabric with a border at each selvedge one of the borders needs to be cut away so that the pattern is correct. The fabric width is therefore made narrower (*fig. 35*), so remember to take this into account when estimating the width of fabric required to obtain the necessary fullness for the curtains.

When making curtains, whether they are unlined, lined or interlined, always prepare the side and bottom hems first. The curtains are then sized up to the required finished length and the heading applied afterwards.

Unlined Curtains

(1) Cut out the curtains, matching the patterns carefully. Cut off selvedges. Where more than one width is necessary in each curtain, joins should be made using a flat fell seam (*fig. 22*).

(2) For the side hems, fold and tack 1.3 cm (½ in) double hems, i.e. making the turning the same size as the hem (*fig. 36*). Machine stitch, ensuring a firm edge to the curtain. The width of the hem can be varied to suit the fabric, e.g. if using a striped fabric make sure that this is folded to finish with a complete stripe or set of stripes.

(3) To make the bottom hem, fold up 5 cm (2 in) at the lower edge of the curtain in order to have a 2.5 cm (1 in) double hem (*fig. 36*). Tack. This hem can then be machine stitched, taking care to keep a neat finish on the right side of the curtain. For heavier fabrics the hems can be hand stitched.

Fig. 36 *Making a 1.3 cm (½ in) double hem at each side edge and a 2.5 cm (1 in) double hem at the lower edge of an unlined curtain*

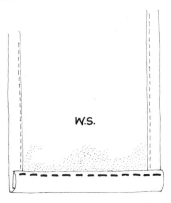

Fig. 37 *Folding in 3.8 cm (1½ in) at the sides and lower edge of a lined curtain*

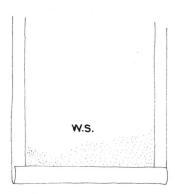

(4) Make a heading or apply tape as required (*see Chapter 8*).

Lined Curtains

To prepare the curtain:

(1) Cut out the curtains, matching any patterns carefully. Cut off all selvedges where necessary (*see page 47*).

(2) Join widths or half widths together with a plain seam (*fig. 20*) and press open. There is usually no need to neaten the edges unless the fabric frays very badly.

(3) Fold in 3.8 cm (1½ in) at the sides and lower edge of the curtain (*fig. 37*). When using a striped or bordered fabric make sure that this is folded to finish with a complete stripe or set of stripes, or folded in an appropriate position in the case of a border.

(4) Mitre the two lower corners and slipstitch *(fig. 25)*. Folded mitres are used on the hems of lined and interlined curtains as they give a neat finish and make the curtains hang well. Mitres can be perfect only when the two hems are the same width.

To make a mitred corner:
   (a) Fold in the two hems the same width of 3.8 cm (1½ in) and press (*fig. 38i*).
   (b) Open out the hems so that they are flat and the press marks are visible (*fig. 38ii*).

1 A Roman blind in a plain cotton gives a sophisticated modern look.

2 A festoon blind made in a co-ordinating sheer fabric.

3 Swags and floor-length tails in silk, lined in a contrasting fabric. The festoon blind in silk faille is drawn up to show the hand stencilled Holland blind, the design of which is repeated on the cushions.

4 A gathered frill and a tie-back used on a floor-length bedroom curtain.

(c) Fold over the right side of the corner onto the wrong side of the fabric to make the first part of the mitre (*fig. 38iii*). Press.

(d) Fold the hem again at the side and lower edge to complete the mitre (*figs. 38iv and 38v*). Slipstitch the two folds together by hand.

(d) If a thick fabric is being used, cut away some of the mitre to achieve a smoother finish. Cut away the fabric from A to B as in fig. 38 iii.

(5) Using matching single thread, serge stitch the two side hems and the lower hem (*fig. 39*).

To prepare the lining:

(1) Cut the lining sateen to the same size as the curtain fabric, removing all selvedges. As lining sateen is not evenly woven it is not possible to pull a thread to straighten the edge, so square it up on a table or use a set square. Do not try to tear it.

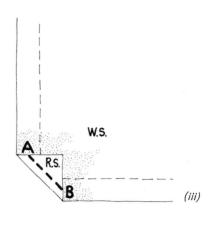

(iii)

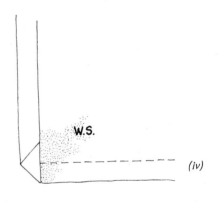

(iv)

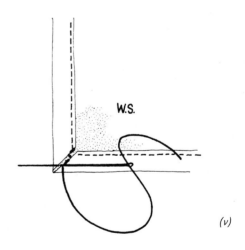

(v)

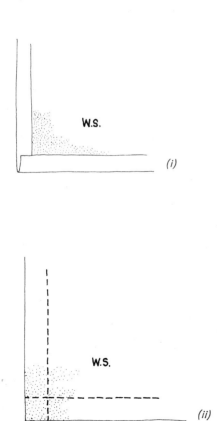

(i)

(ii)

Fig. 38 *(i) Folding and pressing hems to make a mitre (ii) Hems opened flat to show press marks (iii) Folding the corner to make the first part of the mitre (iv) Folding in the side hem (v) Bottom hem folded to complete the mitre and the two folds slipstitched together*

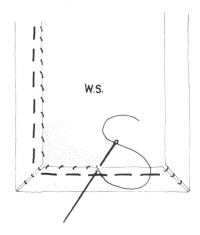

W.S.

Fig. 39 *Serge stitching the side and lower hems on a lined curtain*

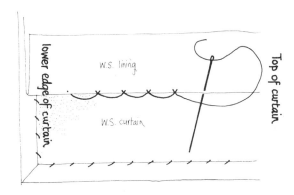

lower edge of curtain

W.S. lining

W.S. curtain

Top of curtain

Fig. 40 *Working a row of locking stitches from the lower edge of the curtain to the top edge*

(2) Lock the lining to the curtain fabric to ensure that it hangs well and does not fall away from the curtain fabric. Locking stitches are long loose stitches made so that they do not pull and pucker the curtain. Two or three rows of locking stitches are made in every width of 122 cm (48 in) fabric. Match the thread to the curtain fabric and not to the lining, and if possible match the seams of the lining to the seams of the curtain fabric.

Fig. 41 *Lined curtain showing rows of locking stitches worked down the length of the curtain*

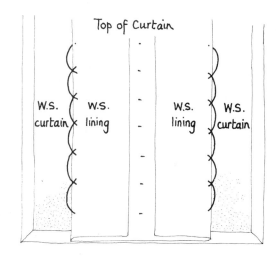

Top of Curtain

W.S. curtain · W.S. lining · W.S. lining · W.S. curtain

Fig. 42 *Lining sateen tacked to the curtain fabric and matching the mitres*

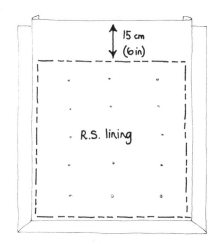

15 cm
(6 in)

R.S. lining

(2) Join widths or half widths as necessary, using a plain flat seam. Press seams open. Half widths on the lining sateen should match as closely as possible the half widths on the curtain fabric.
To apply the lining to the curtain:

(1) Press the curtain carefully and place on a large table with the wrong side uppermost. Press the lining and apply it to the curtain with wrong sides together, matching the seams of the lining to the seams of the curtain where possible. The raw edges of the lining sateen should be flush with the curtain at the lower edge and an equal amount of lining should extend at each side of the curtain.

(3) Fold back the lining at the centre of the curtain and lock into position (*fig. 40*), making the stitches every 10–15 cm (4–6 in). Make another row of locking stitches half way between the centre and the side edges of the curtain (*fig. 41*), or more rows where more than one width is being used.

(4) Trim off the lining sateen at the side edges of the curtain so that it is flush with the curtain.

(5) Fold in the lining 2.5 cm (1 in) at the lower edge and at the two side edges making sure that the corner of the lining meets the mitre on the curtain (*fig. 42*). Tack round the two sides and lower edge.

(6) Work a row of tacking stitches across the curtain 15 cm (6 in) from the top edge. This keeps the lining firmly in position while the heading is worked.

(7) Slipstitch the lining to the curtain at the two sides and lower edge (*fig. 42*) using matching thread. Leave the top 15 cm (6 in) of the curtain unstitched to allow for the heading to be finished.

(8) Make a heading, or apply tape as required (*see Chapter 8*).

Once the curtains have been hung on the track or pole they should be 'dressed'. To do this, set the curtains into even folds, 'breaking' the fabric between each set of pleats forward from the track so that they are proud of the pleats. Smooth the fold evenly down the length of the curtain, then put two or three soft ties round (*fig. 43*). If possible leave the curtains tied for two or three days before using, in order to set the heading or pleating.

Interlined Curtains

(1) Cut out the curtain fabric and the lining sateen as for lined curtains.

(2) Cut the interlining to the same size as the curtain fabric and join widths and half widths as necessary. As bump or domette (see *Glossary* and p. 31) tend to stretch, make the join with a lapped seam using two rows of zig-zag machine stitching (*fig. 44*).

(3) Place the curtain fabric on a large table with the wrong side uppermost. Lay the interlining on the wrong side of the curtain, matching sides and lower edges. Fold back the interlining at the centre of the curtain and lockstitch into position as for lined curtains (*fig. 40*), making three rows of locking stitches to every width of 122 cm (48 in) wide fabric.

(4) Turn in 5 cm (2 in) at each side of the curtain and at the lower edge, folding both the interlining and the curtain fabric together. Mitre the two corners, cutting away the interlining if the corner is too bulky (*fig. 38iii*). Tack and herringbone stitch the hems into position to make a firm edge (*fig. 45*). Slipstitch the mitred corners.

Fig. 43 *Tying up the curtains with soft ties to make the headings set well*

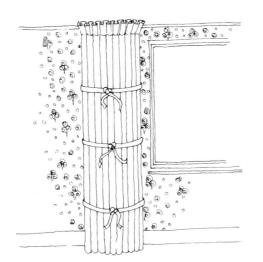

Fig. 44 *Joining interlining fabric with a lapped seam and two rows of zig-zag stitching*

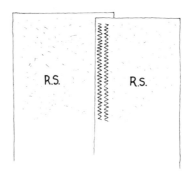

R.S. R.S.

Fig. 45 *Interlining locked to the curtain; stitching the interlining to the curtain fabric using herringbone stitch*

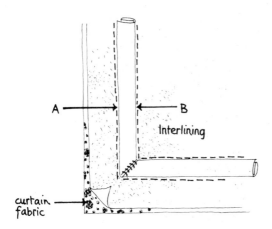

Fig. 46 *Wadding mitred and oversewn into position: Tacking line A shows the finished edge of the curtain; tacking line B is used when applying decorative braid to the right side of the curtain*

(5) Place the lining on top of the interlining, right side up, and work rows of locking stitches as for lined curtains.

(6) Fold in the lining 3.8 cm (1½ in) at the side and lower edges of the curtain, matching mitres, and finish as for lined curtains.

(7) Make the heading or apply tape as required. If the heading is too bulky to pleat, the interlining can be cut off to the required depth of the heading at the top of the curtain. The heading can then be stiffened with buckram when a hand-made heading is chosen (*see Chapter 8*).

Making a wadded edge

An attractive rolled edge can be given to interlined curtains by padding the side hems and the lower hem with synthetic wadding. This produces a thick luxurious edge to the curtain and also helps to prevent the pile from wearing on the hems of velvet and velveteen curtain fabric. It is also extremely effective when used in conjunction with a decorative braid applied to the leading edges of the curtain (*see Chapter 14*). Use synthetic sheet wadding to make the wadded edge. It should be sewn to both side hems as well as to the lower hem as this makes the curtains interchangeable. These curtains must be dry cleaned only, and need careful treatment.

(1) When the interlining has been locked to the curtain, but before the two sides and lower edge are turned over to make the hem, a 5–7.5 cm (2–3 in) border of wadding is applied to the wrong side of the curtain. In order to cover the wadding a 7.5–9 cm (3–3½ in) allowance must be made at the sides and lower edge of the curtain and this must be allowed for at the bottom edge when cutting out the curtains. The wadding must then be prepared so that it fits into this allowance.

(2) Make a line of tacking stitches down the sides and lower edge of the curtain to indicate the position of the fold of the hem. If decorative braid is being applied to the finished curtains make another row of tacking stitches 12.5–15 cm (5–6 in) in from the edge of the curtain (*fig. 46*).

(3) Prepare the wadding by cutting strips 18 cm (7 in) wide by the length required; fold into three lengthwise and tack (*fig. 47*). Mitre the corners by cutting and butting them together. Oversew loosely to hold them into position.

(4) Fold over the side and lower hems of both curtain and interlining to cover the synthetic wadding. Mitre the corners and tack and herringbone stitch into position over the wadding (*fig. 48*).

(5) Finish the curtain by applying and stitching the lining sateen as for lined curtains (*page 48*)

but turning it to leave a 5–6.4 cm (2–2½ in) border all round.

(6) Make the heading or apply tape as required. Cut away the wadding at the top of the curtain to avoid extra bulk.

The width of the wadded edge is dependent upon the type of fabric being used and the size of the curtains and can be varied to suit individual requirements.

Detachable Linings

Loose detachable linings are simple to make and can be added to existing curtains if necessary. They are made quite separately from the curtains, having their own special tape which is attached to the curtain by the same hooks which suspend the curtain itself from the track. They are easily removed for washing and are interchangeable from one set of curtains to another, which makes them useful when different curtains are used for summer and winter. They can be economical too, as they do not necessarily require the same amount of fabric as the curtains themselves. They can usually be made with only one and a half to twice the width of the track.

It is important to remember, however, when considering their advantages and disadvantages, that detachable linings, although useful in some situations, do not have the same professional quality as locked-in linings. They do not enhance the curtains in the same way because they are not locked and permanently sewn to the curtain fabric, and therefore do not drape and hang so well.

(1) Make up unlined curtain as on page 48.

(2) Cut the lining to the same size as the curtain (or one and a half to twice the width of the track) but make the lining 2.5 cm (1 in) shorter than the finished curtain measured from the bottom hem to the heading tape.

(3) Make up the lining by machining 2.5 cm (1 in) double hems at the sides and lower hem and leave the top edge unfinished.

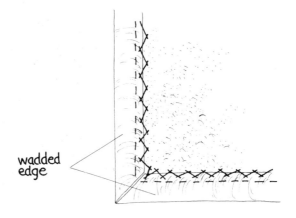

wadded edge

Fig. 48 *Stitching the side and lower hems in position over the wadded edge with herringbone stitch*

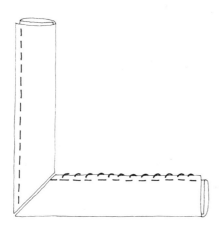

Fig. 47 *Preparing the wadding by folding into three and oversewing together*

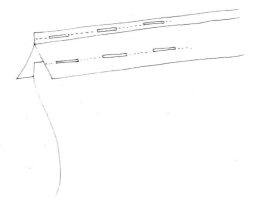

Fig. 49 *Applying a special tape for a detachable lining*

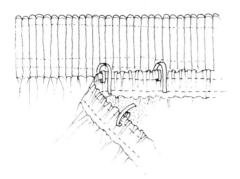

Fig. 50 *Using a detachable lining*

(4) At one end of the lining tape pull out 3.8 cm (1½ in) of cord and knot the ends. Cut off the surplus tape to within 6 mm (¼ in) of the cord. Turn under the end of the tape and stitch across the fold to neaten and secure the knotted ends.

(5) With the right side of the lining facing, place the lining tape, cord side uppermost, between the two sides of the tape (*fig. 49*). Tack into position. Neaten the other end of the tape as above, but leave the cords free for gathering up the lining.

(6) Machine the lining tape into position along the top and bottom edges.

(7) Draw up the cords so that the lining matches the width of the curtain. Attach hooks first into the small hole at the top of the lining tape and then through to the pocket of the curtain heading tape and turn over in the usual way (*fig. 50*).

Café Curtains

These can be one, two or three separate pairs of curtains hung over one window. They can be tailored or dressy and are particularly useful where an unpleasant view needs to be screened or when privacy is required. They look well with other curtains, roller blinds, valances and pelmets and are a good alternative to sheers or nets.

With two-tier café curtains the top pair can be drawn back during the day to let in maximum light, the lower pair remaining drawn across the window.

They are very effective when made in small prints or ginghams and could have a matching valance or pelmet to cover the track at the top.

Single café curtains are usually hung from a metal or wooden pole or rod, so headings for these curtains should be chosen with this in mind. Simple wooden dowelling rods can be painted, stained or varnished, or more decorative metal or wooden curtain poles can be used.

Café curtains can be either unlined or lined, with unlined curtains allowing the maximum amount of light to filter through.

Café curtains are constructed in the same way as lined and unlined curtains, and any of the commercial tapes can be used. Alternatively, a scalloped or tab heading can be made in which case very little fullness is required. This will show the shaped top to advantage.

Making café curtains with a scalloped heading
This is a heading frequently used on café curtains since these are usually hung on rods and not on tracks. It is very decorative and can be made plain or pleated. For plain scallops approximately one and a half times the width of the rod should be allowed, but for pleated scallops more fabric will be required. It can also be used for lined curtains. Make sure that the fabric used is firm.

To make an unlined café curtain with a scalloped heading follow the instructions below:

(1) Prepare the curtain as for an unlined curtain (*page 48*).

Fig. 51 *Planning a scalloped heading*

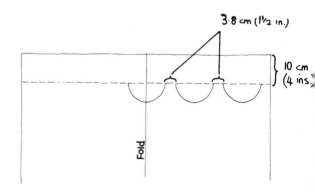

Fig. 52 *Café curtains*

(2) Allow approximately one and a half times the width of the track for this heading. Less fullness is necessary for this heading in order to show up the shaped top. Fabrics lacking body, therefore, are not recommended.

(3) To work out the scallops, prepare a pattern by cutting a piece of paper the width of the curtain and approximately 30.5 cm (12 in) deep. Draw a straight line across the paper 10 cm (4 in) from the top edge, and fold the paper in half (*fig. 51*).

(4) Draw a scallop at the fold line at the centre of the paper and continue drawing scallops along the guide line working outwards to the

side of the paper. Use a plate or compass for this and leave 3.8 cm (1½ in) between each scallop. Leave at least 3.8 cm (1½ in) at each end of the curtain. The number of scallops and their size will vary according to the width of the curtain and the size of the scallop, and adjustments will probably need to be made. When the scallops have been worked out satisfactorily, cut out the paper pattern. For pleated headings, allow more space between each scallop (*fig. 55*) and more width for the curtain depending on the type of pleat used (*see Curtain Headings, Chapter 8*).

(5) With the right side of the curtain uppermost,

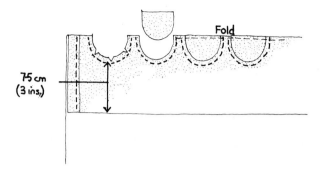

75 cm
(3 ins,)

Fig. 53 *Cutting out the scallops*

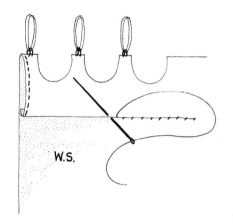

W.S.

Fig. 54 *Stitching the lower edge of the facing*

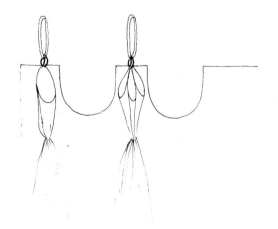

Fig. 55 *Making a pleated scallop*

fold over the top of the curtain to the depth of the scallop, plus 7.5 cm (3 in) for a hem allowance. Tack (*fig. 53*).

(6) Place the paper pattern to the folded edge and mark round the scallops using tailor's chalk. Remove the pattern. Tack and machine stitch on the marking line and cut out scallops 6 mm (¼ in) from the stitching line. Clip corners and curves to avoid puckering when the seams are turned inside.

(7) Turn the facing over to the wrong side of the curtain and press well.

(8) Finish the lower edge of the facing with a 1.3 cm (½ in) hem and slipstitch (*fig. 54*).

(9) Sew rings onto the top of each scallop using buttonhole thread, then suspend the rings from the rod or pole. Alternatively sew on hooks to the back or each scallop and hook into rings on the rod or pole.

For pleated scallops allow more space between each scallop (*fig. 55*) and form the pleat in the space between each scallop. More width will be needed for the curtain depending on the type of pleat used (*see Curtain Headings, Chapter 8*). The pleats are constructed in the same way as for hand-pleated headings.

Making a curtain with a tab heading
This is a heading mostly used for café curtains but it can also be used as an attractive heading when hanging full-length curtains on decorative poles. The following instructions are for making an unlined curtain with a tab heading. On lined curtains it is necessary to insert loops at the top of the curtain between the lining and the curtain fabric. Loops can also be made from decorative braid of a suitable width.

(1) Prepare the curtain as on page 48 but tack a 1.3 cm (½ in) double hem at the top edge.

(2) Work out the number of loops needed at the top of the curtain and mark their positions. Measure round the pole or rod to obtain the length needed for the tab.

(3) For a loop 6.4 cm (2½ in) (finished) and 23 cm (9 in) long (finished) cut a strip of fabric 15 cm (6 in) wide and 25.5 cm (10 in) long. This allows 1.3 cm (½ in) turnings. Fold the strip in half lengthwise with right sides together, tack and machine with 1.3 cm (½ in) turnings. Leave the ends open (*fig. 56*).

(4) Turn the strip to the right side and press, keeping the seam in the centre of the strip on the back of the tab (*fig. 57*). Turn in the raw edges of the strip 1.3 cm (½ in) and press.

(5) Apply the tabs to the wrong side of the curtain, tacking carefully into the marked positions (*fig. 58*). On the right side of the curtain, machine stitch 6 mm (¼ in) all along the top edge. Suspend the loops from the curtain rod or pole (*fig. 59*).

A tab heading can also be made by following the instructions for a scalloped heading, but extend the straight edge 10.0–12.5 cm (4–5 in) above the top of the paper pattern. Cut out and face the scallops as before, but turn over on to the top of the wrong side of the curtain to make a loop. Stitch into position (*fig. 60*).

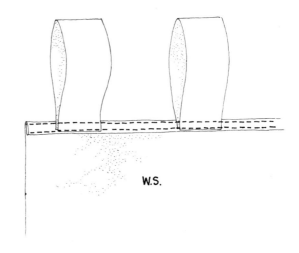

Fig. 58 *Stitching the loops into position on a curtain heading*

Fig. 56 *Making a loop for a curtain heading*

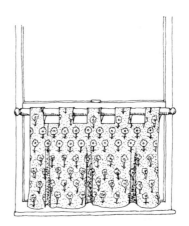

Fig. 59 *Curtain with a tab heading*

Fig. 57 *Making a loop for a curtain heading, showing the seam at the centre back*

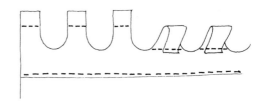

Fig. 60 *Making a tab heading*

Nets and Sheers

Man-made fabrics are normally used for these curtains because they are easy to wash and do not shrink. They can be used when it is necessary to screen the room from the outside without keeping out the light or the view. For the most pleasing effect choose voiles or fine nets, or printed sheers to complement the main curtain fabric. Many are made from polyester and linen and have more body than traditional nets. These voiles can be used together with shutters where the need for lined curtains is not so important. However, blinds could be used instead to give privacy and warmth.

Nets and voiles can be fixed on rods at both the top and bottom of the window, and this keeps them taut and holds them firmly in position. The top rod is fixed on to brackets at the sides of the window and slipped through a casing at the top edge of the curtain. At the lower edge the rod is slipped through a casing at the bottom hem and is secured by a hook at each side of the window. The hooks are then turned slightly to prevent the rod from springing out.

Nets and sheers are made in the same way as unlined curtains but more fullness must be allowed if the fabric is very lightweight. For nets and voiles allow two and a half to three times the width of the track or window. These fabrics are made in several widths from 122–150 cm (48–60 in). This obviates the necessity for seams, which are never made in net or voile curtains as they would show. The side edges do not normally require a hem, but 23 cm (9 in) should be allowed for hems at the top and bottom of the curtain. Turn up a 7.5 cm (3 in) double hem at the lower edge, tack and machine. If making a casing

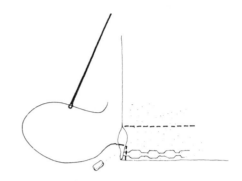

Fig. 62 *Inserting leadweight tape into the hem of a sheer curtain*

for a rod, make another row of machine stitching 2.5 cm (1 in) from the lower edge (*fig. 61*). For man-made fibres use a synthetic thread and a fine needle. Alternatively, leadweight tape can be inserted into the bottom hem of sheers and voiles to improve their draping qualities. Secure this with a few tacking stitches at each end (*fig. 62*).

Turn over 7.5 cm (3 in) at the top edge of the curtain and make a 3.8 cm (1½ in) double hem. Machine stitch along the bottom of the hem and work another row of machine stitching 1.3 cm (½ in) from the top edge to form a casing for the rod.

Alternatively, sheers can be treated in the same way as lined curtains, using pleated headings but always using synthetic tape on synthetic fabrics. Tie-backs can be made from the same fabric or from the same lace or trimming that decorates the curtains.

Shower Curtains

These are constructed in the same way as unlined curtains (*page 48*) but they do not require as much fullness. Shower curtains are usually fixed by hooks and rings from a pole or decorative rod, or they can hang from a special ceiling mounted curtain track (*fig. 64*).

Use nylon showerproof fabric for making these curtains, or waterproof plastic fabric sold especially for this purpose. Alternatively, light cotton curtains that match the decor of the room can be lined with the nylon showerproof fabric, for this is easier to sew than the waterproof plastic material.

Fig. 61 *Making a casing at the lower edge of a sheer curtain*

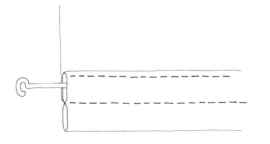

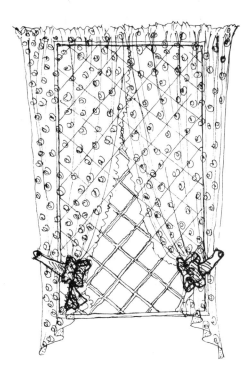

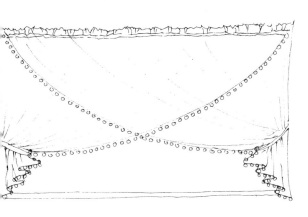

Fig. 63 *Nets and sheers*

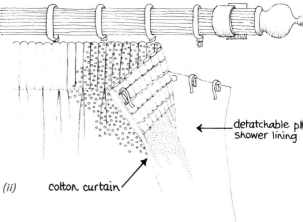

(ii)   cotton curtain

detatchable pl
shower lining

Fig. 64 *(i) Hanging shower curtains from a ceiling-mounted track (ii) Shower curtains using detachable plastic lining*

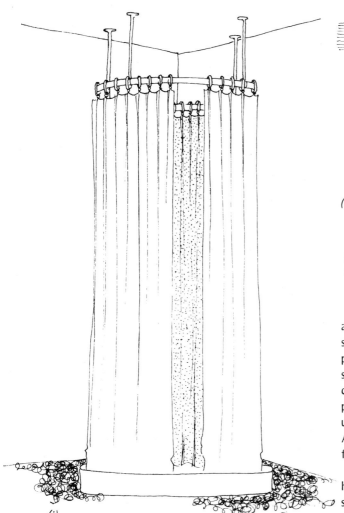

(i)

When sewing plastic fabric use synthetic thread and a long loose stitch when machining, and French seams for joining widths of fabric together. Do not pin or tack the fabric as this would damage it. Hold seams in place if necessary with sticky tape or paper clips. If the fabric is very shiny and does not slide properly beneath the presser foot, use tissue paper underneath the fabric to prevent it from sticking. Alternatively, spread a little talcum powder on the fabric to lubricate it through the machine.

Choose a synthetic heading tape for the curtain heading and hang the curtains from rings from the shower rail or decorative rod round the bath or shower.

8
Curtain Headings

The use of decorative curtain headings has become very popular in recent years and new curtain tapes are often introduced. These are a great help to the curtain maker as they are quick and easy to apply. Before the introduction of such a variety of tapes it was necessary to make decorative headings by hand. Commercial tapes have now enabled people to make their own pinch-pleated headings as well as goblet, smocked and pencil-pleated heads. The hooks can easily be removed for washing or dry cleaning, whereas hand-made headings usually need to be dry cleaned because of their construction.

The pleating or gathering by commercial tapes is usually achieved by pulling up cords in the tape or by inserting special pleater hooks into the tape at regular intervals. Single, double and triple pleats can be made with such hooks. Generally speaking, the use of pleater hooks gives a crisper effect than that produced by tapes that are simply pulled up with cords.

Hand-made headings give a really professional look to a pair of curtains, a valance or a blind. They have the advantage of being made specifically to suit individual requirements, the pleating or gathering complementing the pattern of the fabric. They are often less expensive, as commercial heading tapes and pleater hooks can add considerably to the cost of the curtains. They are, of course, more time consuming to work, but for those who enjoy hand sewing their construction should present few problems.

Commercial Heading Tapes

Gathered heading
This standard pocketed tape, 2.5 cm (1 in) wide, produces a simple gathered heading suitable for use under pelmets or valances where the heading does not show. It can also be used on simple lined or unlined curtains when only a narrow frill is required above the heading. For a really crisp finish, a strip of stiffening such as iron-on bonded interfacing or buckram can be inserted into the fold at the top of the curtains before the tape is applied.

This tape can be obtained in both cotton and man-made fibres for use with lighter fabrics and nets and sheers. Allow at least one and a half times the width of the track when estimating for the curtain fabric.

To apply the tape without a frill:

(1) Measure the width of the curtain to obtain the amount of tape required and allow 2.5 cm (1 in) turnings at each end.

(2) Size up the curtains by measuring from their lower edge to obtain the correct position for the tape, taking the measurement to the curtain ring position on the track or pole. Measure along the curtain every 30.5 cm (12 in) to obtain an accurate result. For a curtain without a frill the tape is sewn in position 6 mm (¼ in) from the top edge, any extra fabric being turned in at the top (fig. 65). Such curtains can then be lengthened, if necessary, by removing the tape and extending from the top edge, thus avoiding a mark at the lower hem.

(3) Cut the heading tape to the width of the curtain plus 2.5 cm (1 in) for turnings at each end.

(4) Tack the heading tape into position at the top edge of the curtain, turning in 1.3 cm (½ in) of tape at each end to neaten (fig. 66). Pull out the cords at each end and knot together.

(5) Machine along the top and bottom edges of the tape and along the two ends (fig. 66). When machining tapes to curtains always stitch along the top edge of the tape first. Take out of the machine and make the second line of stitching

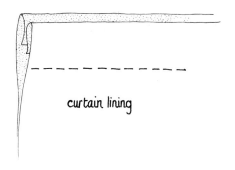

Fig. 65 *Turning fabric in at the top edge of the curtain to allow for ease in lengthening*

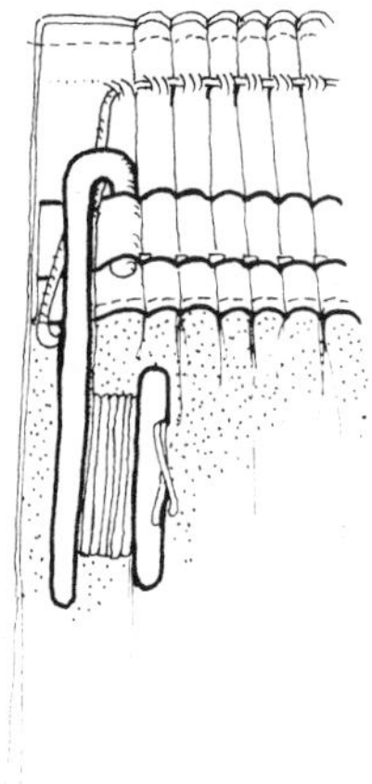

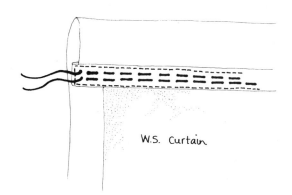

Fig. 67 *Using a cord tidy*

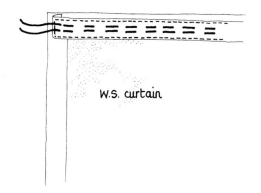

Fig. 66 *The heading tape machine stitched into position*

Fig. 68 *Applying the tape to make a frill at the top of the curtain*

at the lower edge of the tape in the same direction. This prevents the heading from puckering and produces a more even result.

(6) Insert hooks into the tape approximately every 7.5—10 cm (3½—4 in) and draw up the cords on the outside edge of the curtain, distributing the gathers evenly. Do not cut off the cord, but tie neatly into a large bow, or use a cord tidy (*fig. 67*). These can then be released easily for washing or dry cleaning of the curtains.

To apply the tape with a frill:

(1) Measure the width of the curtain to obtain the amount of tape required and allow 2.5 cm (1 in) turnings at each end.

(2) Size up the curtains to obtain the correct position for the tape and allow 5—7.5 cm (2—3 in) extra in length in order to make the frill.

(3) Tack the heading to the top edge of the curtain, covering the raw edges. Fold over onto the lining to the depth of the frill required, which is usually about 2.5—5 cm (1—2 in) (*fig. 68*). To make a stiffer heading cut a piece of interfacing or bonded interlining and insert it into the fold at the top of the curtain (*fig. 69*). Pin, tack and machine stitch all round the tape and finish as in fig. 68.

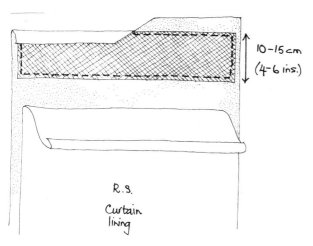

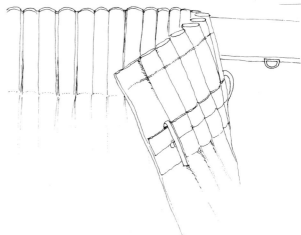

R.S.

Curtain
lining

Fig. 69 *Stiffening tacked into position at the top of the curtain*

Fig. 70 *Pencil pleating tape with pockets positioned at the lower edge of the tape so that the curtain covers the track*

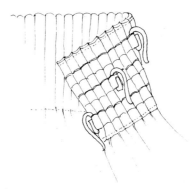

Fig. 71 *Pencil pleating tape showing three different suspension points*

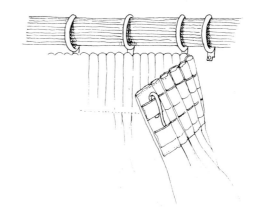

Fig. 72 *Pencil pleating tape showing two different suspension points and the curtain in this case hanging below the pole*

Pencil pleats

Pencil pleats are produced by drawing up cords on specially stiffened tape, and require two and a half to three times the width of the track or pole. The tape is approximately 7.5 cm (3 in) deep and is made in cotton and man-made fibres to suit both heavy and lightweight curtain fabrics.

To apply the tape:

(1) Sew the tape to the curtain 6 mm (¼ in) from the top edge and apply it as for a gathered heading without a frill (*see page 61*). Make sure that the tape is applied with the pockets in their correct position according to whether or not the track or pole is to show above the curtain heading (*fig. 70*). Some tapes have staggered pockets, giving two or three different suspension points (*figs 71 and 72*).

(2) Pull up the cords to make pencil pleats and distribute the gathers evenly.

Pinch pleats

Attractive pinch pleats can be achieved by using one of the several tapes available. These tapes also stiffen the heading. With some tapes the pleats are formed automatically by drawing up the cords, leaving a space between each set of pleats (*figs 73 and 75*). Other tapes have pockets all along it, the width of the curtain being reduced and pleated by the insertion of special long-pronged pleater hooks into the

63

pockets (*fig. 74*). When using this tape it is important to work out the approximate width down to which the fabric will pleat. The following table gives a guide, but it is best to pleat up the tape before applying it in order to work out the formula for the individual curtain. Arrange the hooks so that there is a single pleat at each end of the curtain. The rest of the hooks should be spaced out evenly across the curtain. Use four-pronged hooks for making triple pleats, three-pronged hooks for making double pleats and two-pronged hooks for making single pleats.

When estimating fabric requirements remember that these tapes use two to two and a half times the width of the track according to the tape used and whether single, double or triple pleating is required. Most of the pinch-pleat tapes are available in both cotton and synthetic fibres for use with either heavy or lightweight fabrics.

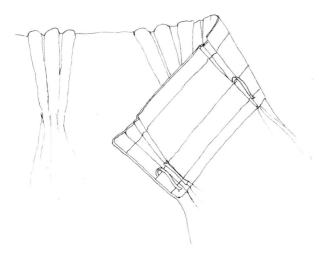

Fig. 73 *Pinch pleated heading; pleats are made automatically by pulling up the cords of the tape*

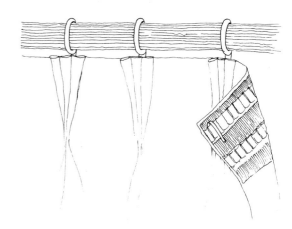

Fig. 75 *Pinch pleated heading hanging below the curtain pole*

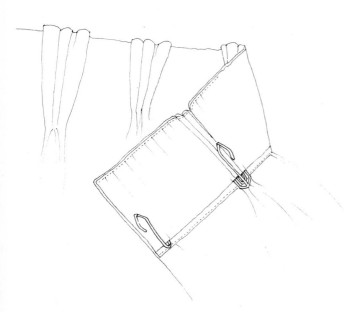

Fig. 74 *Pinch pleated heading; pleating up the curtain with special pleater hooks*

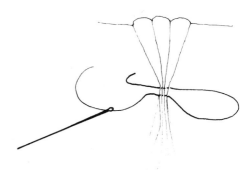

Fig. 76 *Securing the base of the pleat with a few hand stitches*

	Single pleats	Double pleats	Triple pleats
122cm (48 in) fabric pleats down to:	66 cm (26 in) using 9 hooks	61 cm (24 in) using 7 hooks	58.5 cm (23 in) using 6 hooks
183 cm (72 in) fabric pleats down to:	99 cm (39 in) using 14 hooks	96.5 cm (38 in) using 10 hooks	81.5 cm (32 in) using 8 hooks
244 cm (96 in) fabric pleats down to:	135 cm (53 in) using 19 hooks	127 cm (50 in) using 14 hooks	109 cm (43 in) using 11 hooks

These measurements allow 3.8 cm (1½ in) for side hems and approximately 2.5 cm (1 in) for joining widths and half-widths together.

These measurements allow 3.8 cm (1½ in) for side hems and approximately 2.5 cm (1 in) for joining widths and half-widths together.

To apply the tape:

(1) Sew the tape on to the curtains 6 mm (¼ in) from the top edge and follow the instructions for a gathered heading without a frill (*page 61*). Make sure that the tape is applied with the pockets in their correct position.

(2) When using tapes that pleat up automatically by pulling up the cords, the effect of the pleats will be improved by securing the base of the pleat or set of pleats with a few stitches by hand (*fig 76*).

Cartridge and goblet pleats

This tape produces cylindrical pleats which can also be made to resemble goblets (*figs. 77 and 78*). The pleats are formed automatically by pulling up the cords in the tape; no special pleater hooks are required. Two sets of pockets are provided on the tape so that the heading can either cover the face of the track or hang below the pole or track. This ensures that the tape cannot be sewn on to the curtain the wrong way up.

Because cartridge tape makes the curtain drape into neat folds rather than gathers it is also a good choice when used on full-length curtains under pelmets or valances. However, it is more costly

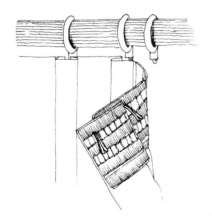

Fig. 77 *Making cartridge pleats by pulling up the cord on the tape*

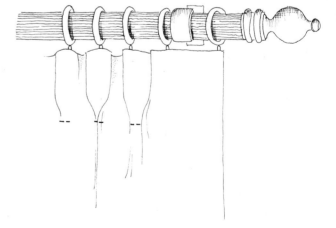

Fig. 78 *Goblet-shaped pleats made by pinching in each pleat at its base and securing with a few stitches*

than the standard pocketed tape which is normally used in this situation. The heading itself does not, of course, show.

To apply the tape:

(1) Sew the tape on to the curtains 6 mm (¼ in) from the top edge and follow the instructions for a gathered heading without a frill on page 61.

(2) Draw up the cords on the tape to make cylindrical pleats. To make a goblet pleat, pinch in each pleat at its base and secure with a few stitches by hand (*fig 78*). Fill the opening of each pleat with a little cotton wool or tissue paper to hold it firmly in position.

(i)

Hand-made Headings

Hand-made headings give a really professional look to a pair of curtains, a valance or a blind (*figs 79–85*).

With hand-made headings the top of the curtain usually needs to be stiffened with buckram or interlining. Special buckram 10–15 cm (4–6 in) wide is obtainable for this purpose, or heavyweight non-woven interfacing can be used. The stiffening should be tacked in to the top of the curtain in the correct position before the heading is worked. Cut the buckram or interfacing to the width of the finished curtain and to the depth of the heading required. Tack into position as in fig. 69. Alternatively, use an interfacing or buckram that can be ironed on to the curtain fabric. Great care is needed when using this as it is not easy to remove once it has been ironed in position.

For those with a little time and imagination the following headings can be used to create original designs for curtains, blinds and valances, which can be adapted to suit individual requirements. The cost of having these made professionally is very high and it is worth mastering the techniques.

French pleats

This is sometimes called pinch pleating, and consists of sets of triple pleats with a flat section in between. It is very decorative and should not be used under a pelmet or valance as it would not show.

When estimating the amount of curtain fabric required allow two to two and a half times the width of the track. Space the pleats 10–12.5 cm (4–5 in) apart and allow 15 cm (6 in) for each set of pleats

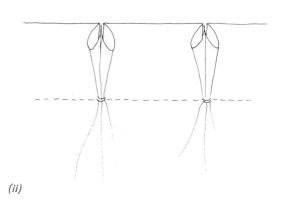

(ii)

Fig. 79 *French pleats (i) Triple pleats – allow 15 cm (6 in) for each set of pleats (ii) Double pleats – allow 10 cm (4 in) for each set of pleats*

with a space of 7.5 cm (3 in) at each end of the curtain.

To make the heading:

(1) Prepare the curtains as for lined curtains (*page 48*).

(2) Stiffen the heading (*fig. 69*) and turn in and press the top of the curtain and lining 2.5 cm (1 in). Tack and slipstitch.

(3) Mark out the pleats and spaces along the top edge of the curtain with pins and tailor's chalk, using fig. 86 as a guide. The size of the space between each set of pleats may need to be adjusted to fit the width of the curtain.

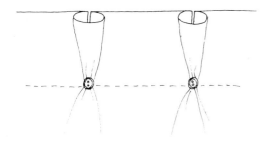

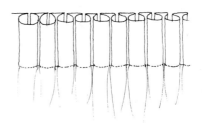

Fig. 83 *Pencil pleats*

Fig. 80 *Single pleats trimmed with a decorative button*

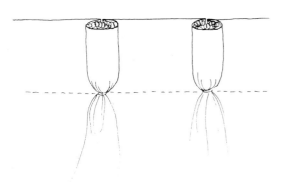

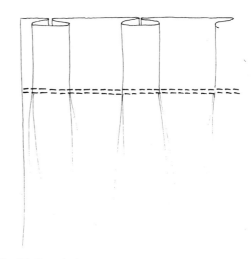

Fig. 84 *Box pleats*

Fig. 81 *Goblet pleats*

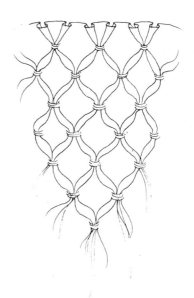

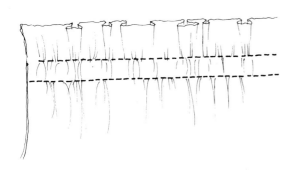

Fig. 82 *Gathered heading*

Fig. 85 *Smocked heading*

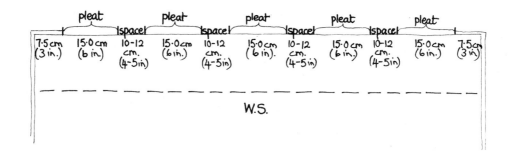

W.S.

Fig. 86 *Planning French pleats (triple pleating)*

(4) Mark and pin a 15 cm (6 in) pleat 7.5 cm (3 in) from the left-hand side of the curtain and one 7.5 cm (3 in) in from the right-hand side of the curtain, folding each pleat with the wrong sides together. Next, find the centre of the curtain by folding pleat 1 to pleat 2, and pin in pleat 3. Similarly, fold pleat 1 to pleat 3 to find the centre of pleat 4, and pin into position. Fold pleat 3 to pleat 2 to find the centre of pleat 5, and pin into position (*fig. 87*).

(5) Tack and machine each pleat from the top of the curtain to the bottom of the stiffening (*fig. 88*). Divide this pleat into three small ones, allowing 5 cm (2 in) for each pleat. Oversew the pleats together at point A and stab stitch through them back to the point where they join the curtain (*fig. 89*).

(6) Secure the pleats at the top of the curtain with a few oversewing stitches (*fig. 88*).

(7) You can use stab-in single pronged hooks for hand-made headings, inserting them upwards into the centre back of each pleat or group of pleats. They can easily be adjusted if the top of the curtain is not absolutely straight or the length needs altering (*fig. 90*). Alternatively, cut a piece of plain heading tape the length of the finished heading plus 2.5 cm (1 in) for turnings and pin and tack to the wrong side of the curtain. This tape is approximately 3.8 cm (1½ in) wide and looks rather like webbing tape. Hem stitch all round the tape and sew a hook to the tape behind each set of pleats, also sewing one 2.5 cm (1 in) from each side of the curtain. Use buttonhole stitch for extra strength.

Double pleats can be made instead of triple, the method being exactly the same, but allow 10 cm (4 in) instead of 15 cm (6 in) for each set of pleats.

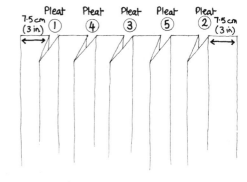

Fig. 87 *Working out the position for the pleats*

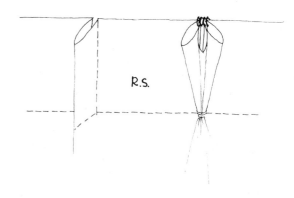

Fig. 88 *Folding the heading to make French pleats*

Single pleats

Single pleats can be made instead of French pleats, and they take much less material — an advantage when using expensive fabrics. Patterns also show up better when there is less fullness. Allow approximately one and a half times the width of the track. Space the pleats 9–10 cm (3½–4 in) apart and make each pleat 5–7.5 cm (2–3 in) with a space of 7.5 cm (3 in) at each end of the curtain.

The method for making single pleats is the same as for French pleats. The single pleat is tacked and machined from the top of the curtain to the bottom of the stiffening, as in fig. 88. The pleat is then pinched in and oversewn at point A (fig. 89).

A single-pronged hook is then inserted into the back of the curtain behind each pleat (fig. 90). Alternatively, sew on heading tape and hooks as in fig. 91.

Single pleats look very effective if decorated with covered buttons in matching or contrasting fabric or with suitably tied bows to match the curtain fabric.

Goblet pleats

Goblet pleats are similar to single pleats but take more fullness. They are made larger than single pleats and are padded out to make a goblet shape. Allow twice the width of the track for this type of pleating. Space the pleats 10 cm (4 in) apart and make each pleat 10 cm (4 in) with a space of 7.5 cm (3 in) at each end of the curtain.

To make the heading:

(1) Prepare the curtain as for lined curtains and stiffen the heading (fig. 69).

(2) Mark out the pleats and spaces along the top edge of the curtain following the directions for French pleats.

(3) Fold, tack and machine each pleat from the top of the curtain to the bottom of the stiffening with wrong sides together.

(4) Pinch in the pleat at the bottom and oversew into position. Stabstitch through the pleat back to the point where it joins the curtain. Open the pleat at the top of the curtain to make a rounded shape, and secure by oversewing to the top of the curtain as in fig. 92. Fill the opening of the goblet pleat with cotton wool or tissue paper to hold it firmly in place.

(5) Use single stab-in hooks and stab them into the back of the curtain behind each pleat, or sew on heading tape and hooks as in fig. 91.

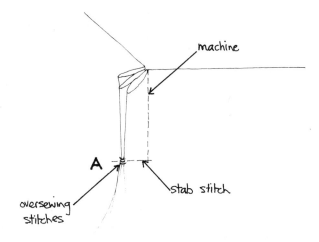

Fig. 89 Securing the pleat with stitching

Fig. 90 Stab-in single-pronged hooks used in the back of a hand-made heading

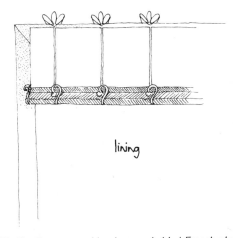

Fig. 91 Heading tape and hooks sewn behind French pleats

69

Gathered heading

The construction of the curtain is as for lined or unlined curtains (*see pages 48-50*) but the heading is made to fit the pole or track precisely. When calculating fabric for this heading allow one and a half to twice the width of the track to obtain the necessary fullness.

To make the heading:

(1) Take the measurement of the track and divide it into two. Add 7.5 cm (3 in) for each overlap of the curtain at the centre of the window. The heading is then gathered up to finish to this measurement (*see example in fig. 93*).

(2) Turn over the amount needed for the heading: 1.3 cm (½ in) if under a pelmet, 5–6.4 cm (2–2½ in) if a frill is required.

(3) Divide the width of the curtain into four equal sections and mark with tailor's chalk or pins. Gather each section separately with two rows of running stitches 3 mm ($\frac{1}{8}$ in) apart (*fig. 94*).

(4) Cut a piece of plain heading tape the length of the finished heading plus 2.5 cm (1 in) for turnings (*fig. 95*). Divide into four equal sections, turning in 1.3 cm (½ in) at each end of the tape.

(5) On the wrong side of the curtain pin the tape to the fabric matching tailor's chalk marks or pins, and gather up the curtain to fit into each section of the tape. Secure each section of gathering round a pin (*fig. 96*).

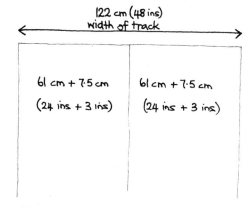

Finished width of each curtain to be 68.5 cm (27 ins)

Fig. 93 *Planning a hand-made gathered heading*

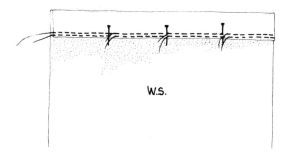

Fig. 94 *Gathering each section separately*

Fig. 95 *Preparing the heading tape for a gathered heading*

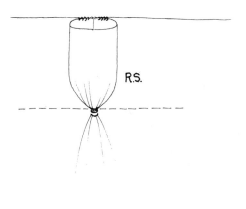

Fig. 92 *Oversewing the goblet pleat to the top of the curtain*

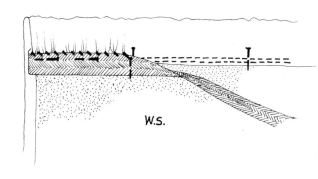

Fig. 96 *Applying the heading tape to a gathered heading*

70

(6) Hem along the top edge of the tape picking up each gather separately using strong thread or buttonhole twist for heavy curtains.

(7) Turn the curtain to the right side and adjust each gather along the lower edge of the heading tape. Stitch using a small backstitch between each gather.

(8) On the wrong side of the curtain sew hooks onto the tape using buttonhole stitch, securing at top and bottom edges and using buttonhole twist for extra strength. Space the hooks 6.4–7.5 cm (2½–3 in) apart, and sew them on 1.3 cm (½ in) in from each end of the curtain (*fig. 97*). Alternatively, use stab-in single-pronged hooks (*fig. 90*).

Pencil pleats

This is a gathered heading using evenly spaced stitches that makes small rounded pleats like pencils lined up one against the other. Instead of small stitches, as in the simple gathered heading, larger stitches are used on the wrong side of the curtain with smaller ones on the right side. When the gathers are drawn up, large pencil pleats are formed on the right side. It looks well on tall windows, when the heading can be made as much as 15 cm (6 in) deep. Allow three times the width of the track when estimating curtain fabric for this heading.

To make the heading:

(1) Prepare the curtain as for lined curtains, and stiffen the heading (*fig. 69*). Fold in the top of the curtain and the lining 2.5 cm (1 in).

(2) Cut the heading tape to the required finished measurement.

(3) At the top and bottom edges of the heading or stiffening draw two horizontal guide lines with tailor's chalk. Also make vertical guide lines 2 cm ($\frac{7}{8}$ in) apart so that the stitches match up and are exactly opposite to one another (*fig. 98*).

(4) Using a long length of buttonhole thread make a row of stitching along each guide line, making 1.5 cm ($\frac{5}{8}$ in) stitches on the wrong side of the curtain and 6 mm (¼ in) stitches on its right side.

(5) Pull up the gathering threads adjusting the pleats to the length of the heading tape. Sew on the heading tape to the wrong side of the curtain, hemming along the top edge and sewing in

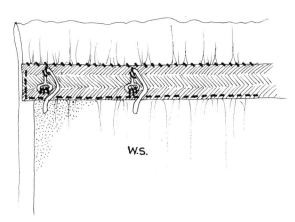

Fig. 97 *Curtain hooks sewn to the back of a gathered heading*

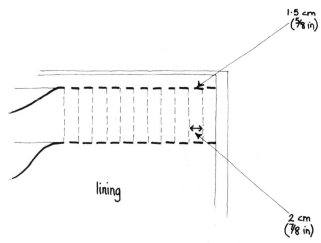

Fig. 98 *Making horizontal and vertical guide lines before stitching*

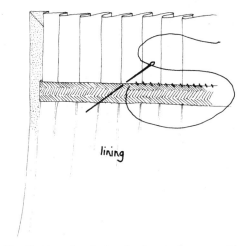

Fig. 99 *Hemming the heading tape to the wrong side of the curtain*

71

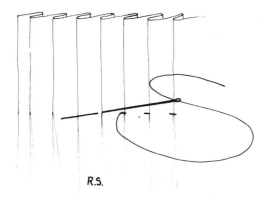

R.S.

Fig. 100 *Making a backstitch between each pleat*

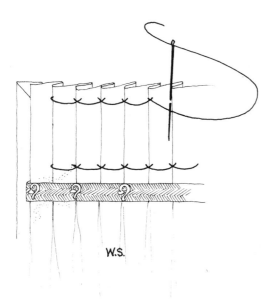

W.S.

Fig. 101 *Lockstitch used to hold the pleating in position*

each pleat separately (*fig. 99*). Turn to the right side of the curtain and stitch the bottom edge of the tape to the curtain, using a small back-stitch between each pleat (*fig. 100*). Sew hooks onto the tape about 10 cm (4 in) apart, or use single-pronged stab-in hooks.

(6) To hold the pleating firmly in position make a lock stitch along the top edge of the curtain (*fig. 101*). Another row of lock stitching can be worked if the heading is very deep.

Box pleats

Small box pleats make a dainty heading for curtains as well as festoon blinds and valances. For the following small pleats allow twice the width of the track when estimating the curtain fabric required. This allows a 3.8 cm (1½ in) pleat with 10 cm (4 in) from the centre of one pleat to the centre of the next. The heading can be made from 2.5–10 cm (1–4 in) deep depending on its purpose.

To make the heading:

(1) Prepare the curtain as for lined curtains and only lightly stiffen the heading.

(2) Measure out and mark for pleating as in fig. 102. Pin and tack each pleat, and machine into position. Flatten the pleats out against the curtain to form the box pleat and tack into position (*fig. 103*).

Fig. 102 *Measuring and marking for box pleats*

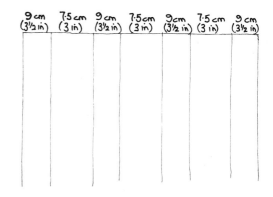

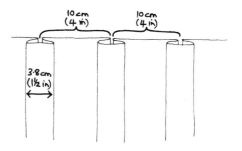

5 Full-length curtains and valance match the drapes on the bed.

6 Contrasting bows and tie-backs used effectively on a simple pair of curtains.

7 Festoon blind made in cotton fabric and bound with a contrasting colour co-ordinates well with the wallpaper in this small country bathroom.

(3) Tack and machine along the bottom of the pleating. Press (*fig. 104*).

(4) On the wrong side of the heading slipstitch each pleat through to the lining to prevent the pleat from falling forwards.

(5) Cut a piece of plain heading tape the length of the finished heading and apply it to the wrong side of the curtain at the lower edge of the pleating (*fig. 105*). Sew hooks on to the tape 2.5 cm (1 in) from each end of the curtain and behind each box pleat, or use stab-in single-pronged hooks.

When making box-pleated valances hold each pleat firmly in position by making a buttonhole bar on the wrong side of the valance at the bottom hem (*fig. 106*).

Fig. 103 *Making the box-pleated heading*

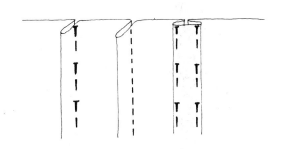

Fig. 104 *Tacking box pleats into position*

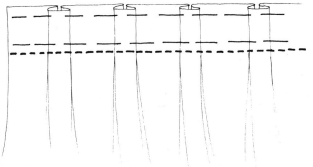

Fig. 105 *Applying the heading tape to the lower edge of the pleating*

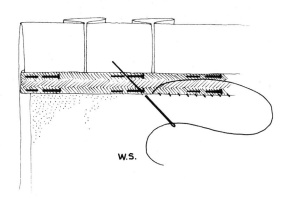

W.S.

Smocked heading

Although a commercial 'smocked' heading tape is available, genuine hand smocking worked on curtain headings and valances is most attractive. Instructions are given here for a honeycomb stitch. Allow approximately three times the width of the curtain for this heading. Other decorative smocking stitches could be used instead of honeycombing, and this heading gives scope for those who like doing traditional smocking.

To make the heading:

(1) Cut the heading tape to the required length.

(2) The smocking is formed by rows of even gathers, and it is essential that these gathers are evenly worked. To do this, make five horizontal lines of dots along the position for the heading (*fig. 107*), making sure that each is exactly below the one above. Sheets of dots for smocking can be obtained from craft shops, but they can also be marked out by hand. If a checked fabric such as gingham is used, the checks can be used as guides. The length of each stitch depends to some extent on the fabric in use, but for a curtain or a valance they should not usually be less than 1.3 cm (½ in), as the effect would be lost if the gathering stitch were too small.

(3) Gather each row of dots and draw up firmly to straighten each fold (*fig. 108*). Secure the ends of the gathering thread round a pin.

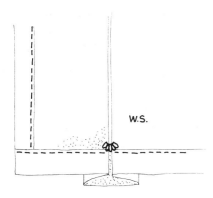

W.S.

Fig. 106 *Making a buttonhole bar on a box pleated valance*

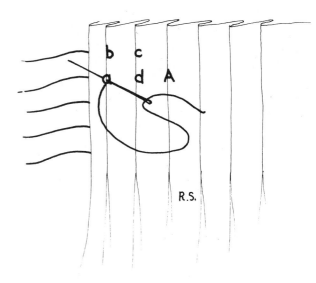

R.S.

Fig. 108 *Gathering the fabric for a smocked heading and working the honeycomb stitch*

(4) Starting at the second row of gathering stitches, and working on the right side of the curtain from left to right, pick up and work one stitch at (a), which is the first pleat. Take the thread to (b), and made another stitch. With the thread above the needle make another stitch at (c), which is the second pleat. Keeping the thread above the needle, pick up another stitch at (d). With the thread below the needle take up a stitch at A. This is the beginning of the next group of stitches (*fig. 108*).

(5) Continue along these two rows and work the next rows in the same way.

(6) When the honeycomb stitching is completed take out the gathering thread.

(7) Sew on the heading tape to the wrong side of the curtain as for a gathered heading, adjusting the smocking to fit. Sew on hooks, or use single-pronged stab-in hooks.

W.S. lining

Fig. 109 *Stitching the tape to the strip of lining fabric*

Fig. 107 *Marking out a smocked heading*

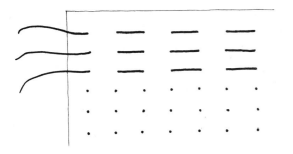

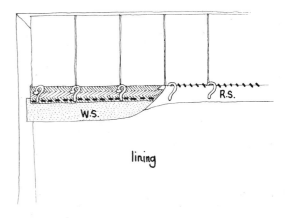

R.S.

W.S.

lining

Fig. 110 *Neatening the heading tape with a strip of lining fabric*

Neatening the heading tape on hand-made headings

On lined curtains with hand-made headings, and where a heading tape with sewn-on hooks has been used, a very neat finish can be obtained on the wrong side of the curtain by covering the heading tape with a strip of the curtain lining fabric.

(1) Cut a piece of curtain lining sateen from selvedge to selvedge and 1.3 cm (½ in) larger all round than the finished length of the heading tape.

(2) Before applying the tape to the curtain, turn in the tape 1.3 cm (½ in) at each end, tack and machine stitch the wrong side of the lining strip to the tape (*fig. 109*).

(3) Apply the heading tape to the wrong side of the curtain and sew the hooks onto the tape.

(4) Fold up the lining strip to cover the tape, and slipstitch along the top edge of the tape under the shank of the hook (*fig. 110*).

Sheer curtains with a frilled edge.

9
Blinds

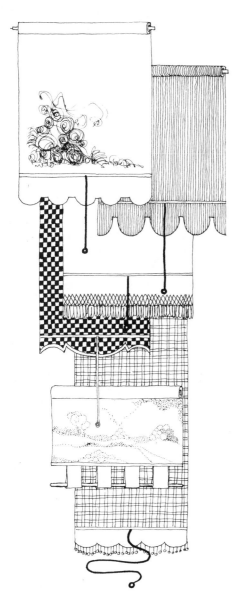

Roller Blinds

Roller blinds are easy and inexpensive to make at home and they are more practical than curtains in kitchens and bathrooms. They roll right up to the top of the window to give the maximum light by day.

Roller blind kits are obtainable at do-it-yourself shops and many large stores. Special Holland fabric should be used to make the blind, as this is quick and easy to use and does not fray at the edges. It repels dirt and dust and can be sponged clean. It is made in wide widths, so joining is often unnecessary.

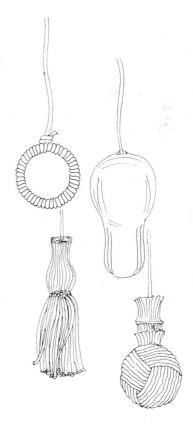

Fig. 111 *Some ways of finishing roller blinds*

Closely woven furnishing cottons and linens can also be used for making roller blinds but need to be strengthened first with a fabric stiffener. This can either be sprayed on to the fabric from an aerosol can, or the fabric can be dipped into a special liquid stiffener (usually obtainable where roller blind kits are sold). Test a small piece of fabric first to check how much stiffening is required.

Make the blind from one width of fabric if possible. For a wide window the fabric can be used sideways if the pattern allows. If necessary make two or even three blinds for a very wide window. Seams in a blind are not always satisfactory as they make the fabric too thick and stop the roller from working smoothly. With commercially stiffened fabrics that do not fray it is not necessary to have side hems as this also adds thickness to the blind. However, if a fabric stiffener is used it is sometimes necessary to turn in the side hems 1.3 cm (½ in) and machine into position using a zig-zag stitch (or two rows of straight stitch). When machining, keep the fabric as flat as possible as the stiffened fabric can crack if folded.

The lower edge of the blind may be finished in one of many ways (*fig. 111*). A shaped edge can be made and fixed to the bottom edge, or a decorative braid or fringe can be used. Pull cords can be obtained in various styles, or a hand-made knotted or plaited cord could be applied.

Fig. 113 *Roller blind decorated with fabric paint using a stencil design*

Plain blinds can be decorated with fabric paints using free-hand designs or stencils (*fig. 112*). These are most effective as they can be designed to co-ordinate with tiles, fabrics etc. in the room. Stencils in many designs can be purchased for this purpose and are made of paper or plastic. A stencil brush should be used to apply the special fabric paint, which can be obtained from good art and craft shops.

Fig. 112 *Roller blinds decorated with fabric paints using free-hand designs to match the tiles*

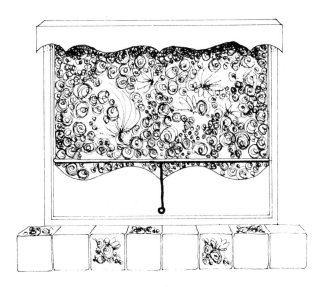

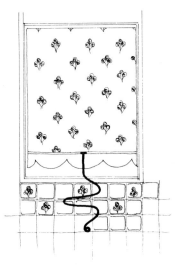

Fig. 114 *Versatility of roller blinds*

Secure the stencil firmly to the blind using double-sided sticky tape or masking tape before painting on the design. Practise stencilling first on a small piece of blind fabric before painting the design on the blind itself.

In measuring the window decide whether the blind is to be fixed inside or outside the window recess (*fig. 115*). If a kit cannot be obtained in the exact size buy the next size up and trim the roller down to the size required.

A kit consists of a wooden roller which has a spring and metal cap with a rectangular pin at one end of the roller. Another metal end cap with a round pin is provided to fit onto the other end of the roller when it has been cut to the exact size required (*fig. 116*). Two metal brackets are supplied: one is fixed to the left-hand side of the window to take the spring and rectangular pin, and the other bracket is fixed at the right-hand side of the window and takes the end with the round pin (*fig. 117*). Special tacks are also provided for applying the fabric to the roller. An acorn fitment with tacks and a pull cord is also provided together with a wooden batten to give weight to the bottom hem of the blind.

INSIDE

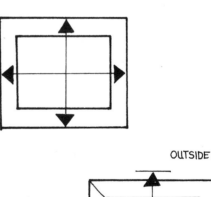

OUTSIDE

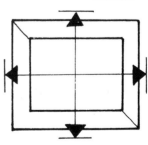

Fig. 115 *Deciding on the position for the roller blind*

79

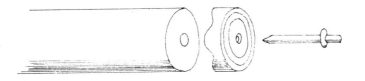

Fig. 116 *Cut the wooden roller to size before fixing the cap with the round pin*

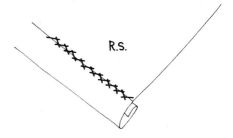

Fig. 118 *Making a casing at the lower edge of the blind*

To make the roller blind:

(1) Cut the wooden roller to the correct size to fit between the two brackets.

(2) Cut the fabric to the exact size of the roller. If hems need to be made at each side a 2.5 cm (1 in) allowance must be made for these. The fabric should be approximately 15 cm (6 in) longer than the measurement of the window. This allows for turnings at the bottom edge of the blind and also enables fabric to be rolled round the roller when it is pulled down. It is very important to cut the fabric accurately, or the blind will not roll evenly. Square up the fabric with the edge of a table, or use a T-square to get accurate angles.

(3) At the lower edge turn up 1.3 cm (½ in) to the wrong side of the blind and then turn over 3.8 cm (1½ in) to make a casing for the wooden batten. Use a little adhesive to hold the hem in place and then machine along the hem using a zig-zag stitch (*fig. 118*).

(4) Position the blind to the roller as in fig. 119, making sure that the right side is uppermost.

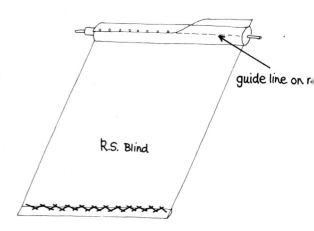

Fig. 119 *Positioning the blind to the roller*

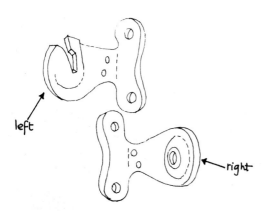

Fig. 117 *Fittings for a roller blind*

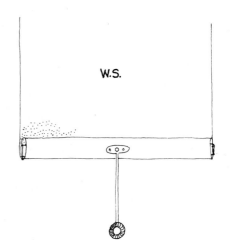

Fig. 120 *Acorn fitting screwed into position*

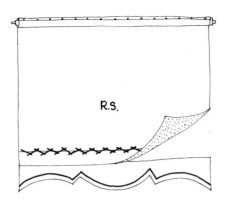

R.S.

Place the fabric to the guide line on the roller and stick down with a little adhesive. Tack down every 3.8 cm (1½ in) along the roller.

(5) Cut the wooden batten to the width of the blind and insert in the casing at the lower edge. Knot one end of the pull cord and thread through the acorn fitting. Screw the fitment to the wrong side of the blind (*fig. 120*).

(6) The lower edge of the blind can be decorated with braid, or a piece of blind fabric can be cut to the shape chosen and fixed to the back of the casing with adhesive (*fig. 121*).

Fig. 121 *Fixing a trimming to the lower edge of the blind with adhesive*

Fig. 122 *Roman blinds*

Roman Blinds

Roman blinds are softer than roller blinds because they pull up the window in soft folds. They should be made from firmly woven curtain fabric and should be lined with curtain sateen. There is no need to stiffen the fabric for this type of blind. Curtain rings are fixed onto cotton or synthetic tape at the back of the blind and cords are then threaded through the rings to enable the blind to be pulled up (*fig. 127*). The blind is attached to a wooden batten approximately 5x2.5 cm (2x1 in) at the top of the window and when pulled up is secured on a cleat hook at one side of the window.

To make the blind:

(1) If the blind is being positioned inside the window recess cut out the fabric to the size of the window and allow 18 cm (7 in) for turnings at the top and bottom hems and 7.5 cm (3 in) for the turnings at the sides.

(2) Cut the lining to the same size as the blind fabric and place wrong sides together. At the side edges turn in both thicknesses of fabric 6 mm (¼ in) and then 1.3 cm (½ in). Tack and press.

(3) Turn up the bottom hem 6 mm (¼ in) and then 10 cm (4 in). Press, but do not stitch.

(4) Mark parallel guide lines down the blind from top to bottom for positions of tape, making the side guide lines 1.3 cm (½ in) in from each edge (*fig. 123*). The lines should be equidistant and about 30.5 cm (12 in) apart.

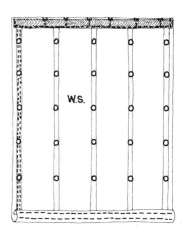

Fig. 124 *Tape stitched into position and rings sewn on at regular intervals; the casing at the lower edge is for the wooden batten*

Fig. 125 *Screw-in eyes positioned on the wooden batten*

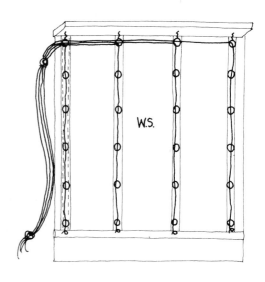

Fig. 126 *Threading cord through the rings and screws on the blind and the wooden batten*

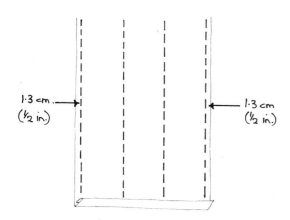

Fig. 123 *Marking parallel guide lines for positioning the tape*

82

(5) Apply 1.3 cm (½ in) wide cotton or synthetic tape to the guide lines as in fig. 124. Tuck the ends of the tape into the hem at the bottom edge and tack into position. Machine stitch along both sides of the tape through both lining sateen and fabric.

(6) Tack and machine the lower hem into position. Make a second row of machine stitching 3.2 cm (1¼ in) down from the first to make a casing for the wooden batten (fig. 124).

(7) Insert the wooden batten into the casing and slipstitch both ends to enclose the batten.

(8) With the blind lying flat, sew small brass or plastic rings into the tape (or use split curtain rings) at regular intervals from 15–30.5 cm (6–12 in) (fig. 124) depending on the width of the fold required.

(9) Turn over the top of the blind 2.5 cm (1 in) and pin a length of plain heading tape to the top of the blind, keeping the tape level with the top edge. Turn in each end of the tape 1.3 cm (½ in). Make two rows of machine stitching at the lower edge of the tape. At the top edge stitch the tape down every 9–10 cm (3½–4 in), using buttonhole thread, to form small pockets (fig. 124). Place a drawing pin in each pocket to attach it to the wooden batten.

(10) At the lower edge of the wooden batten place screw-in eyes to match up with the rings in the tapes (fig. 125). Place a cleat hook at one side of the window, where the blind will draw up. Fix the blind to the wooden batten.

(11) Lay the blind flat and thread strong nylon cord through the rings as in fig. 126. Take the cord up through the rings on each length of tape and then across to one side of the blind, threading it through the screw eyes in the wooden batten. When all the tapes have been threaded up, knot them together 2.5–5 cm (1–2 in) from the last screw eye (fig. 126). Cut the cords so that they are all level and knot again (fig. 126).

(12) Mount the batten and the blind to the window and fix the cleat hook into position. Draw up the blind and tie the cords round the cleat hook (fig. 127).

(13) If desired, the blind can be trimmed with braid, which should be applied to the two sides and the lower edge.

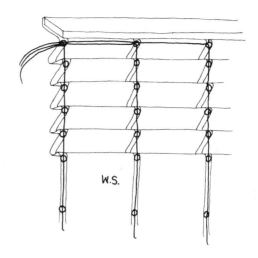

Fig. 127 *Pulling up the Roman blind*

Festoon Blinds

Festoon blinds (sometimes called Austrian blinds) are similar in construction to Roman blinds but require more fabric as they are gathered both across the width and down the length of the blind. They are very fussy and probably best suited to bedrooms and bathrooms. As with Roman blinds, they are fixed to a batten at the top of the window and drawn up by cords and rings attached to the back of the blind. They do, however, have pleated or gathered headings to draw up the fullness across the blind. They are best made from thin, lightweight fabrics that drape well. Lining is optional.

To make the blind:

(1) Decide on the position for the blind and the wooden batten. This can be either inside or outside the window recess. Mount a curtain track on to a wooden batten 2.5x5 cm (1x2 in).

(2) Cut out the fabric for the blind, allowing one and a half to twice the width of the track depending on the fullness required, and one and a half times the length (depth) of the window. To make a frill along the lower edge of the blind cut a strip of fabric 10 cm (4 in) deep and one and a half to twice the fabric width.

(3) Make any joins necessary in the blind fabric widths, using a French seam for an unlined blind. If possible, seams should be made where the tapes will be positioned.

83

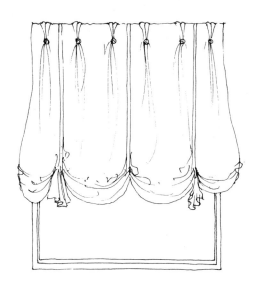

Fig. 128 *Festoon blinds*

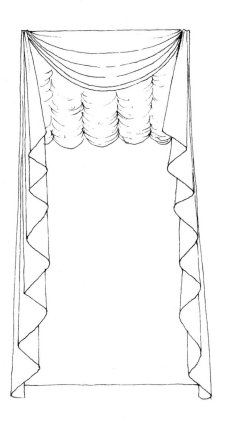

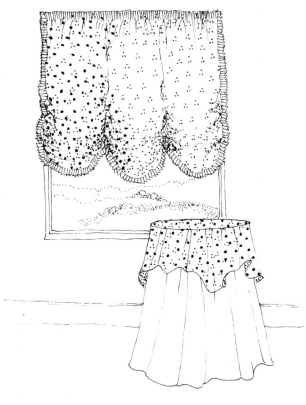

84

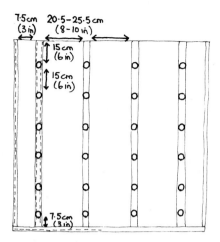

15 cm
(6 in)

15 cm
(6 in)

7·5cm
(3 in)

Fig. 129 *Position of tapes on a festoon blind*

(4) Make 1.3 cm (½ in) double hems at sides and bottom edges.

(5) Mark the positions for the tape, making guide lines 7.5 cm (3 in) in from each side of the blind. The remainder of the guide lines should be equidistant and anything from 20.5–25.5 cm (8–10 in) apart to make attractive swags (*fig. 129*).

(6) Apply standard synthetic pocketed tape to each vertical line, and tack and machine into position. Insert split curtain rings into the tape at regular intervals, approximately every 15 cm (6 in) starting 7.5 cm (3 in) from the bottom hem. Make sure that the rings are positioned evenly across the blind.

(7) Cut out the frill (*see 1 above*) and make a 6 mm (¼ in) double hem on one long side of the fabric and along the two short sides. On the other long side make two rows of gathering stitches 6 mm (¼ in) apart (*fig. 130*). Draw up to fit the bottom edge of the blind. Pin and tack to the wrong side of the blind. Machine into position (*fig. 131*).

(8) Apply curtain heading tape to the top of the blind, turning in the top edge 1.3 cm (½ in). Tack and machine into position. Pull up the tape to fit the width of the track. Alternatively, a hand-made heading can be made following the instructions in Chapter 8.

(9) Draw up the pocketed vertical tape from the top of the blind so that it fits the length of the window, and knot. A frill will then form on each side of the blind.

(10) Thread up the blind with nylon cord in the same way as for the Roman blind (*page 83*) tying each cord to the first ring at the lower edge of the blind.

Fig. 130 *Making a gathered frill for a festoon blind*

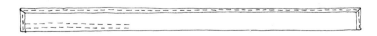

(11) Fix screw eyes to the underside of the wooden batten parallel to the lines of tape down the blind. Insert curtain hooks into the heading tape and fix to the curtain track. Thread the cord through the screw eyes and pull up the blind in festoons.

It may be necessary to sew small weights into the hem of the blind at the bottom of each length of pocketed tape to make the blind hang well.

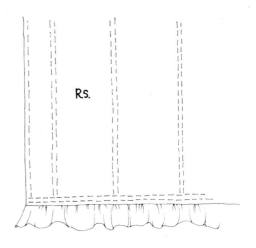

Fig. 131 *Attaching the frill to the lower edge of the blind*

10
Pelmets

Pelmets came into fashion in the seventeenth century and were developed from the valance because of architectural changes in window design. Originally a pelmet was an embroidered strip of fabric, but it was later turned into something very elaborate and ornate, and was used well into the Victorian era. In recent years the trend has been away from pelmets but, in fact when they are well designed,

Fig. 132 *Some designs for pelmets*

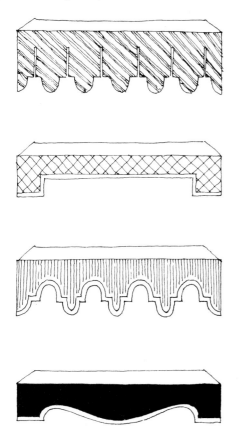

pelmets can add considerably to the interest and originality of a room's decor. They create a decorative finish to the tops of curtains and at the same time conceal tracks and headings. The shape of a pelmet can alter the appearance of a window. It can be fixed higher than the window frame to make the window appear taller, or can be extended at each side to make it appear wider.

When designing a pelmet, care should be taken to make it proportionate to the height of the room and the window. As a rough guide, allow 3.8 cm (1½ in) of pelmet depth to 30.5 cm (12 in) of curtain drop, or one sixth of the total depth of floor length curtains. This should give a well-proportioned pelmet.

A simple design can be as effective as a more elaborate one, and sometimes the pattern of the fabric can suggest a suitable design for the pelmet. Alternatively, try using a design from a chair in the room if it belongs to an interesting period (*fig. 133*).

Pelmets give a look of distinction to a room and are most effective when used with roller blinds or café curtains. They can also be used very successfully when draping dressing tables and beds.

Pelmets are economical to make and they can considerably reduce the cost of curtaining a window,

Fig. 133 *Period styles (i) Regency (ii) Victorian (iii) Edwardian (iv) William and Mary*

(i)

(ii)

(iii)

(iv)

since only a gathered heading is necessary underneath a pelmet (although a commercial cartridge tape could be useful if folds rather than gathers are required). The gathered heading requires less fullness than other decorative headings, and therefore less curtain fabric is needed.

A pelmet is usually made to match the curtains and is mounted on to either an iron-on buckram or to a special pelmet buckram (this is a coarse canvas impregnated with glue). Regular buckram is also suitable and can be used together with an adhesive.

A stiffened pelmet should be fixed to a pelmet board and not on to a 'valance' rail. Pelmet boards should be approximately 10 cm (4 in) deep by 2.5 cm (1 in) thick and should extend 5—7.5 cm (2—3 in) beyond the end of the curtain track. They are fixed like a shelf, using brackets. The height of fixing above the window frame can be varied to suit the effect required. For an average window the board is fixed approximately 5—7.5 cm (2—3 in) above the frame. The pelmet is then attached to the front edge of the board with drawing pins or with Velcro.

Pelmets made with buckram cannot be washed and must be dry cleaned, but regular brushing or vacuuming should keep them in good condition.

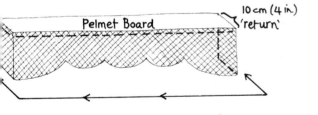

Fig. 134 *Plan of a pelmet showing 10 cm (4 in) 'returns' at each end of the board*

Estimating the fabric

Measure the length of the pelmet board from wall to wall, remembering to include the 10 cm (4 in) returns at each end. To this measurement add 5 cm (2 in) for turnings (*fig. 134*). The depth of the pelmet is determined by the design; allow 3.8 cm (1½ in) pelmet to 30.5 cm (12 in) of curtain drop, or one-sixth of the total depth of floor length curtains. To this measurement add 10 cm (4 in) for turnings. In rooms with low ceilings keep the depth of the pelmet to a minimum, but not usually less than 18 cm (7 in).

Centre the width of the fabric in the middle of the pelmet and add any extra fabric each side of this width; never have a seam at the centre of the pelmet. When estimating the amount of fabric required, remember to allow for pattern matching. The same amount of lining sateen and interlining is needed as for the face fabric. Interlining gives more body to the fabric and a slightly padded look to the pelmet.

Designing the pelmet

(1) Make a template of the design required, bearing in mind the following important points. The position where the curtains will hang when drawn back gives the measurement of the 'end' sections. The return at each end should be the same depth as the 'end' sections. The measurement of the design or scallop must be taken into consideration to enable it to be fitted in satisfactorily. The narrowest part of the pelmet must not permit the track to show when the curtains are drawn back (*fig. 135*).

(2) Make a mark at the centre of the pelmet design and cut out the template in stiff paper or newspaper (strips can be pinned or stuck together) to the full size of the pelmet. Mark out the important measurements described

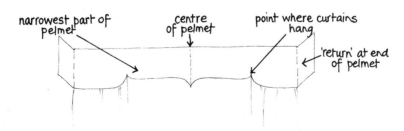

Fig. 135 *Designing the pelmet*

above and start designing the pelmet from the centre, using plates or trays as guides to draw round. Fix the pattern onto the pelmet board with drawing pins or sticky tape and adjust one side of the pattern only until the required effect is achieved. Live with the paper template for a few days before cutting out the final pattern to be sure that it satisfies the eye.

(3) When a satisfactory design has been achieved, fold the template in half and cut the other side to match. The design is then ready to transfer to the pelmet buckram.

(4) If in doubt about a design, keep it simple — or straight. A pelmet can be decorated with a fringe, piping cord, tassels or other decorative edges and this can be more effective than an elaborate design that has been badly planned.

Cutting the buckram

(1) Cut a strip of buckram the exact length of the pelmet board plus the 'returns' at each end, usually about 10 cm (4 in) each. If possible avoid making joins in the buckram, but if it has to be done, join the buckram by over-lapping the two edges 1.3 cm (½ in), and then machine into position.

(2) Lay the paper template on to the buckram and secure it by damping the buckram very slightly and ironing the pattern to it. Cut out the buckram, using a sharp pair of scissors.

Preparing the face fabric

(1) Cut a strip of fabric 10 cm (4 in) larger all round than the exact size of the finished pelmet. This allows for the fabric to be turned over onto the buckram (*fig. 136*).

(2) Join widths of fabric where necessary, keeping a full width of fabric at the centre of the pelmet. Make 1.3 cm (½ in) seams, matching patterns carefully (*fig. 26*). Press seams open.

Applying the interlining

(1) Cut a strip of bump or domette (see *Glossary* and page 31) 5 cm (2 in) larger than the exact size of the finished pelmet, joining the pieces with a lapped seam and two rows of zig-zag machine stitching.

(2) Place the buckram on to the interlining, exactly in the centre. Starting at the top edge of the

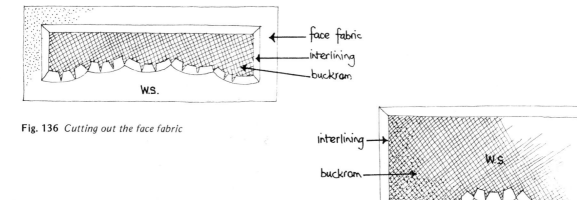

Fig. 136 *Cutting out the face fabric*

Fig. 137 *Applying the interlining to a pelmet*

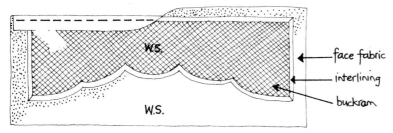

Fig. 138 *The face fabric tacked along the top edge of the pelmet*

pelmet dampen the buckram at the edges with a small cloth. Fold over the interlining and press firmly to the buckram with a hot iron. Continue in this way all round the pelmet, slashing curves and cutting away surplus fabric on the convex curves. Right angled curves also need slashing and the surplus fabric to be trimmed away (*fig. 137*). (When using regular buckram apply a little adhesive to the buckram before folding over the interlining.)

Applying the face fabric

Lay the buckram and the interlining on to the wrong side of the face fabric and tack into position along the top edge making sure that the fabric is correctly positioned on the right side. Fold over the face fabric on to the wrong side of the buckram (*fig. 138*). Dampen the buckram and press down in the same way as for the interlining, slashing curves and mitring each corner and cutting away surplus fabric where necessary. Slipstitch the corners (*fig. 139*). If the fabric frays easily, reinforce each slash with a few buttonhole stitches (*fig. 140*).

Applying the trimming

(1) If a decorative trimming, braid or piping is used it should be applied to the pelmet before the lining is applied.

(2) With the right side of the pelmet facing, stabstitch the trimming to the pelmet using matching thread, and taking care to keep a good line (*fig. 139*).

(3) Furnishing cords or braids can also be used effectively to decorate the face of a pelmet. They should be stitched on and not applied with an adhesive.

Applying the lining fabric and heading tape

(1) Cut a strip of lining sateen 5 cm (2 in) larger than the finished pelmet. Join strips together, if necessary, with 1.3 cm (½ in) turnings, and press seams open.

(2) With the wrong side of the pelmet facing, turn in the lining 1.3 cm (½ in) and pin 6 mm (¼ in) from the top edge of the pelmet. Turn in the sides in the same way.

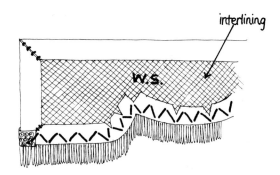

Fig. 139 *Wrong side of pelmet showing trimming applied to the pelmet with stabstitch*

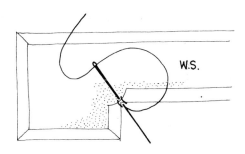

Fig. 140 *Reinforcing a slash with buttonhole stitches*

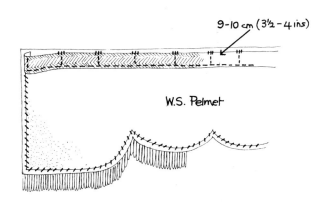

Fig. 141 *Stitching the lining to the pelmet; heading tape in position*

(3) Cut the lining to the shaped edge allowin 2.5 cm (1 in) for turnings and turn in as before slashing curves where necessary. Slipstitch th lining to the pelmet all round (*fig. 141*).

91

(4) Cut a piece of heading tape 2.5–3.8 cm (1–1½ in) wide, the length of the pelmet plus 2.5 cm (1 in) for turnings. Pin the tape to the top edge of the pelmet and turn in 1.3 cm (½ in) at each end. Using matching button-hole thread, backstitch the ends and lower edge of the tape to the pelmet, making sure that the stitches go through to the buckram but not to the face fabric. Stitch the tape down every 9–10 cm (3½–4 in) to form pockets and attach to the pelmet board with drawing pins (*fig. 141*).

(5) Alternatively, a piece of Velcro can be stitched to the back of the pelmet and the matching strip glued to the front of the pelmet board.

(6) Buttons can be covered in the face fabric and applied to the right side of the pelmet for decoration. Alternatively, motifs of patchwork or other decorative embroidery could be used.

11
Valances

A valance is a piece of gathered or pleated fabric used where a soft informal effect is required. Valances are shortened versions of curtains, and any of the hand-made headings and some of the commercial heading tapes can be used to make them. Estimate the amount of fabric required as for curtains (*Chapter 7*). The depth of the valance should be calculated in the same way as for a stiffened pelmet i.e. 3.8 cm (1½ in) of valance per 30.5 cm (12 in) of curtain drop.

Valances are not stiffened with buckram, but they can be interlined with bump (see *Glossary*) or a non-woven interfacing when thinner fabrics are used, or when pleated valances are being made. They should always be lined. The back of the valance should be finished with a curtain heading tape and either hung from a valance rail or attached to a pelmet board with drawing pins or Velcro. The tape should be attached 3.8—5 cm (1½—2 in) from the top of the back of the valance so that it covers the top of the rail or board. This also prevents it from sagging.

Valances can also be used round dressing tables, vanitory units and baths and are effective when making drapes for beds.

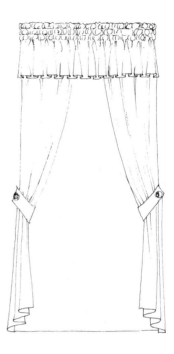

Fig. 142 *Valances (i) Goblet pleating on a valance (ii) Box-pleated valance (iii) Gathered valance (iv) Valance with triple pleats*

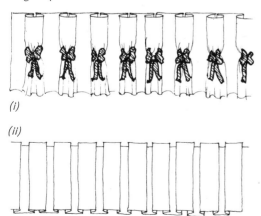

(i)

(ii)

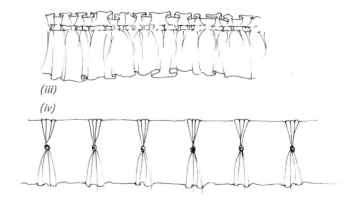

(iii)

(iv)

Gathered Valance

(1) Decide on the depth of the valance and allow 3.8 cm (1½ in) for the bottom hem, 5 cm (2 in) for the heading and 2.5 cm (1 in) at each side edge. A gathered valance needs plenty of fullness, so allow at least double the length of the valance rail or pelmet board (remembering to include the return at each end).

(2) Cut out the fabric and lining and if necessary join widths together using 1.3 cm (½ in) seams and press open.

(3) Make up the valance as for a lined curtain and stitch a strip of standard pocketed curtain tape on to the back of the valance 3.8–5 cm (1–1½ in) from the top edge (fig. 143). Alternatively, pleat up the valance by hand using the techniques described on pages 66-75 and in fig. 144, or make three rows of running stitches as in fig. 145 and gather up the valance by hand. Apply plain heading tape and hooks or Velcro 3.8–5 cm (1–1½ in) from the top of the valance.

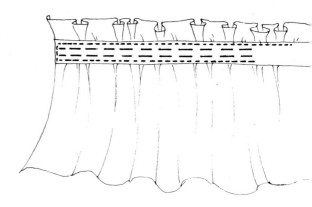

Fig. 143 *Standard pocketed gathering tape attached to the wrong side of the valance 3.8 - 5 cm (1½ - 2 in) from the top edge*

Pleated Valance with Shaped Edge

(1) Decide on the depth of the valance and allow 3.8 cm (1½ in) for the lower hem and 5 cm (2 in) for the heading and 2.5 cm (1 in) at both side edges. Decide on the type of pleating required and estimate the width of fabric needed as for pleated curtain headings (*Chapter 8*). A pleated valance should be interlined.

(2) Cut out the fabric, lining and interlining and join widths together if necessary. On this type of valance the lining forms part of the design, so a careful choice of matching or contrasting coloured lining should be made to complement the face fabric (*figs 146 and 147*).

(3) Before making up the valance work out and mark the positions for the pleating and spacing of the face fabric. Draw scallops along the lower edge of the fabric using a plate as a guide, or use a compass. Have the deepest point of the scallop exactly in the centre of the space between the measurement for each pleat. The narrowest point of the scallop should be at the centre of each pleat (*fig. 148*).

(4) Make up the valance, locking the interlining to the face fabric as for interlined curtains

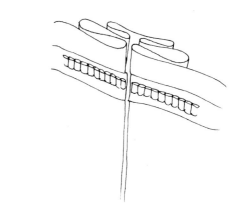

Fig. 144 *Hand-pleated valance*

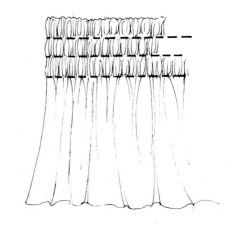

Fig. 145 *Three rows of running stitches used to make a gathered valance*

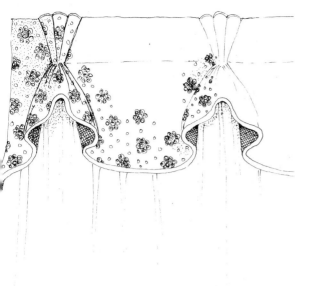
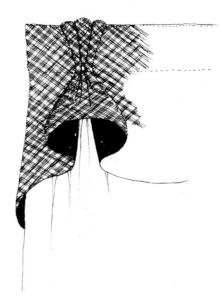

Figs 146 and 147 *Pleated valance with shaped edge; the lining of the valance must complement the face fabric as this forms part of its design*

(*page 51*). Turn in the lining and slipstitch to the top and two sides of the valance. At the lower edge of the valance extra care must be taken to slipstitch the lining exactly to the bottom edge as this will show on the right side when the valance is in position (*figs 146 and 147*).

(5) Insert stab-in hooks at the back of each pleat 3.8–5 cm (1½–2 in) from the top edge of the valance, or use tape and sew-on hooks as for curtains (*Chapter 8*) and hang on to the valance rail. Alternatively, stitch Velcro to the back of the valance and glue the matching strip to the front of the pelmet board.

Fig. 148 *Planning a pleated valance with a shaped edge*

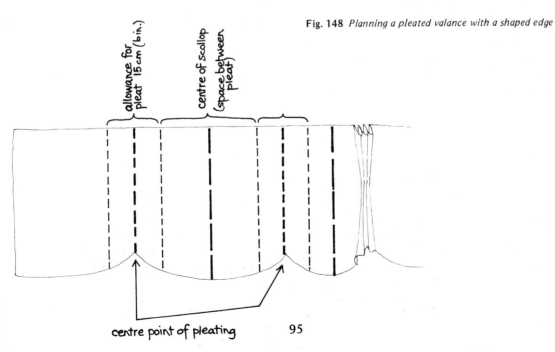

allowance for pleat 15 cm (6 in.)

centre of scallop (space between pleat)

centre point of pleating

Simple curtain style with a festoon blind made in sheer fabric.

12
Swags and Tails

Swags and tails are used where a formal window treatment is required. They are best used in tall, elegant rooms where the furnishings are rather grand. Although they can be varied slightly in style they should always be made in rich looking fabrics such as velvet, brocade, dupion or silk (or its imitations). They can then be decorated with matching braids, fringes and tassels to complete the formal picture. It is important to choose fabric with good draping qualities. Swags and tails are really draped pelmets, which give the appearance of a piece of fabric thrown over a pole at the head of the curtains.

Making swags and tails requires a little practice and some patience. Make a toile (pattern) first, in muslin, cheap cotton or calico to try out the design and size. This is essential as it gives practice and also enables the right effect to be achieved.

The swag is the piece of fabric which is fixed along the whole length of the pelmet board. It must be cut on the cross grain of the fabric and is draped and pleated to a depth of one sixth of the curtain length (as with a stiffened pelmet or valance). A series of swags can be made to fit across the pelmet board and they should overlap each other by 10—15 cm (4—6 in). Alternatively, one large swag can be made, but this can be more difficult as it might be necessary to join fabric widths together.

The tails are fixed at each end of the pelmet board. They should be lined, and then pleated and attached to the pelmet board. Make the tails approximately twice the length of the swag, and cut them on the straight grain of the fabric.

Plan the swags and tails as you would design a pelmet, taking into account the position of the curtains when drawn back and the depth of the window. The lining on the tails will be visible, so choose a colour for the lining that will match or contrast well

with the fabric.

Variations of swags and tails can be made to suit individual windows when a little experience has been gained. However, it is always best to make a toile or mock up in cheap cotton first.

To make a swag:

(1) Cut out the swag on the cross-grain of the fabric to make sure that a good drape is achieved. Use fig. 150 as a guide to measurements and proportions. These proportions apply to most swags and can be adjusted if necessary. Allow 1.3 cm (½ in) turnings all round. Fold in the turning allowance and press.

(2) Mark out the positions for the pleating down each side of the swag, making the spaces approximately 10 cm (4 in) apart (fig. 151).

(3) Fold up the pleats, taking B to A, C to B, D to C and E to D (fig. 152). Pin and stitch the pleats into position when they have been draped satisfactorily.

(4) Cut out the lining to the size of the draped swag and allow 1.3 cm (½ in) turnings all round. Fold down the turning allowance to the wrong side and press.

(5) With the right sides together, pin and tack the top edge of the lining to the top edge of the swag and machine stitch into position (fig. 153). Turn the right sides out, and slipstitch the lining to the curved edge of the swag.

(6) Stitch a piece of heading tape to the top of the swag using buttonhole thread, attaching it as for a stiffened pelmet (page 92). Alternatively, sew on a strip of Velcro (fig. 154).

To make the tails:

(1) Cut out a pair of tails in muslin or cotton first in order to obtain a suitable pattern for the drape. Allow 1.3 cm (½ in) turnings all round.

Fig. 149 *Swags and tails*

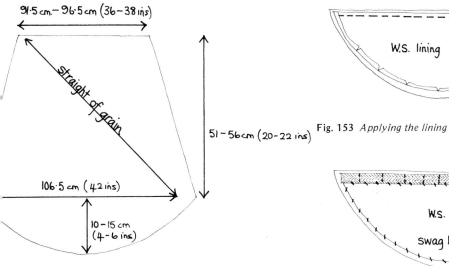

91.5 cm. – 96.5 cm (36 – 38 ins)

straight of grain

51 – 56 cm (20 – 22 ins)

106.5 cm (42 ins)

10 – 15 cm
(4 – 6 ins)

Fig. 150 *Cutting plan for a swag*

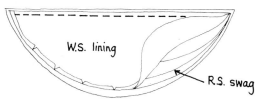

W.S. lining

R.S. swag

Fig. 153 *Applying the lining to the right side of the swag*

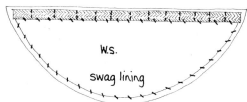

W.S.

swag lining

Fig. 154 *Lining and heading tape slipstitched into position*

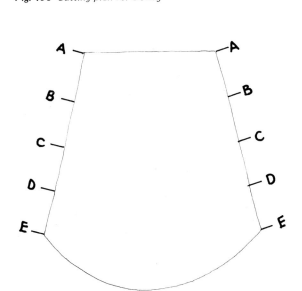

A — A
B — B
C — C
D — D
E — E

Fig. 151 *Positions marked for pleats*

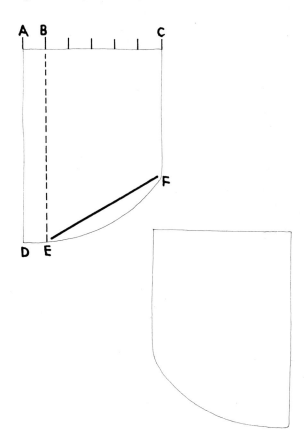

A B   C

D E

F

Fig. 155 *Plan for a tail, showing positions for pleats*

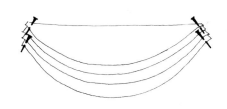

Fig. 152 *Pleating up the swag*

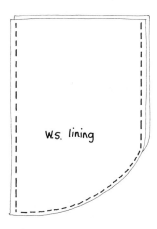
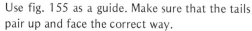

W.S. lining

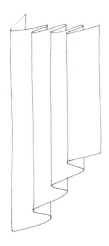

Fig. 156 *The lining stitched to the tail, leaving the top edge open*

Fig. 157 *Tail folded into a cascade of pleats*

Use fig. 155 as a guide. Make sure that the tails pair up and face the correct way.

(2) AD is the depth of the tail at the side of the window. AB is the return at the end of the pelmet board, usually about 10 cm (4 in). This is not pleated. CF is the narrowest part of the tail before pleating. EF can be a straight line or a curve, according to the style required.

(3) Cut out the lining to the exact size of the tail, alowing 1.3 cm (½ in) turnings all round. With right sides facing, pin and tack the lining to the tail, leaving the top edge open (*fig. 156*). Machine stitch into position. Trim seams and clip curves. Turn to the right side, turn in the top edges and slipstitch.

(4) Mark positions for even pleats along the top edge of the tail (*fig. 155*). Fold the pleats into a cascade and stitch into position (*fig. 157*). Apply heading tape or Velcro to the back of the tail as for the swag. Decorate the swags and tails with tassels, rosettes or decorative braids, fringes, etc. These should be sewn on by hand.

100

13
Tie-backs for Curtains

Tie-backs are quick and easy to make and can be very decorative. They are used to hold curtains back from the window, as a rule, and are hooked to a small cleat fixed to the wall or window frame. They can be made from either heavy or lightweight fabrics, and to match or contrast with the curtains. They are usually stiffened with heavy interfacing or pelmet buckram and can be trimmed with braid, piping cord, fringing, binding, etc. or they can be simply made from a piece of ribbon, lace, or plaited cords or fabric (*fig. 158*).

Straight Tie-back Stiffened with Interfacing

(1) Decide on the length and width of the tie-back. To estimate the length, tie a piece of string or a tape measure round the curtain to obtain the right effect (*fig. 158i*). Do not make the tie-back too short as this could cause creasing in the curtains.

(2) To this measurement cut a strip of fabric, interfacing and lining sateen to the length and width required. Add 1.3 cm (½ in) for turnings on the face fabric and the lining sateen. The interfacing is cut to the exact size of the finished tie-back.

(3) Cut the ends of the strips into points or curves if desired (*fig. 159*).

(4) Place the interfacing onto the wrong side of the face fabric. On the face fabric fold over 1.3 cm (½ in) all round onto the interfacing and herringbone stitch into position, mitring each end if necessary (*figs 160 and 161*).

(5) Sew a strong brass or plastic curtain ring to each end of the tie-back, using buttonhole stitch and a strong thread (*fig. 160*).

(6) Place the wrong side of the lining sateen to the wrong side of the tie-back. Turn in the lining so that it finishes 6 mm (¼ in) from the edge of the tie-back. Slipstitch into position (*fig. 162*).

Shaped Tie-back Stiffened with Buckram

(1) Make a paper pattern of a shaped tie-back and experiment with different shapes before cutting out the fabrics, adjusting the pattern until a pleasing effect is obtained (*fig. 158*).

(2) Fold and cut the pattern in half, and using one side only cut out the buckram (*fig. 163*).

(3) Place the paper pattern to the fold of the face fabric and cut out round the pattern allowing 2.5 cm (1 in) turnings all round (*fig. 164*). Cut a piece of interlining (bump or domette) and a piece of lining sateen in the same way but alow 1.3 cm (½ in) turnings all round.

(4) Place the buckram on to the interlining and dampen the edges of the buckram slightly using a small cloth. Fold over the interlining and press firmly onto the buckram using a hot iron (*fig. 165*). Slash curves and cut away surplus interlining at corners if necessary.

(5) With the interlining side facing down, place the tie-back onto the wrong side of the face fabric. Fold over the raw edge of the fabric to the wrong side of the tie-back. Dampen the buckram and press the fabric down using a hot iron. Slash curves and mitre corners where necessary.

(6) Sew on strong curtain rings at each end of the tie-back for straight tie-backs. Place the wrong side of the lining to the wrong side of the tie-back. Turn in 1.3 cm (½ in) all round, clipping curves where necessary and slipstitch into position (*fig. 166*).

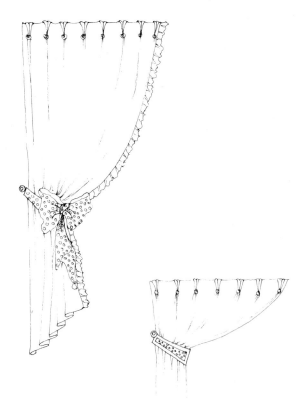

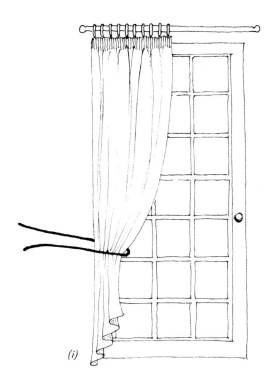

Fig. 158 *Some ideas for tie-backs (i) Taking the measurement for a tie-back*

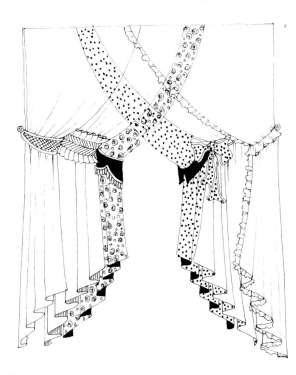

102

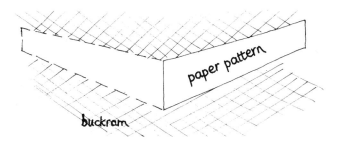

Fig. 159 *Cutting the ends of the tie-backs into points or curves*

Fig. 163 *Cutting out the buckram from the paper pattern*

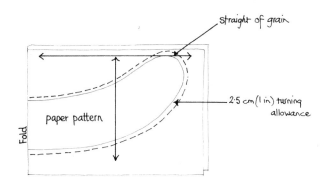

Fig. 160 *Stitching the face fabric to the interfacing; curtain ring sewn into position with buttonhole stitch*

Fig. 164 *Cutting out the face fabric for a shaped tie-back*

Fig. 161 *Mitring the pointed end of a tie-back*

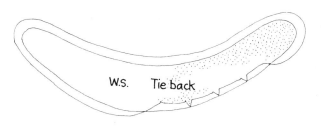

Fig. 165 *Applying the interlining to the buckram*

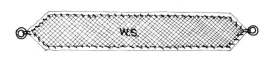

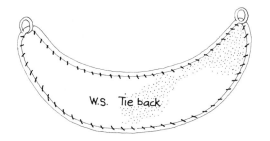

Fig. 162 *The lining slipstitched into position*

Fig. 166 *Lining slipstitched to a shaped tie-back*

Fig. 167 *Preparing a strip of fabric for a plaited tie-back*

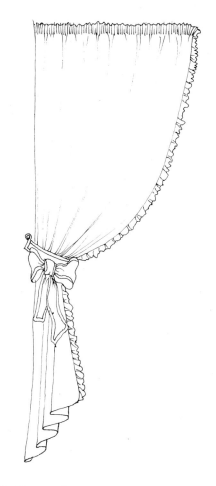

Plaited Tie-back

Plaited tie-backs can be made from narrow pieces of fabric folded and stitched as in fig. 167. Alternatively, thick piping cord looks effective when covered with lengths of crossway strip or bias binding cut in matching or contrasting fabric or in a mixture of each. Follow the directions for cutting on the cross in Chapter 14.

Fig. 168 *Tie-backs for curtains made in matching curtain fabric and decorated with satin ribbon*

Fabric Bow Tie-back

Attractive tie-backs can be made from bows made from the same fabric as the curtains and trimmed with ribbons or binding (*fig. 168*).

(1) Cut a strip of fabric approximately 23 cm (9 in) by the length needed to make a suitable bow. (This varies from 1½–2 meters and obviously depends on the thickness of the curtain to be be tied back.) Measure carefully using a piece of string as in fig. 158i and allow for tying a bow.

(2) With right sides together fold the fabric in half lengthwise and machine stitch along the two long sides (*fig. 169*). Turn right sides out and press. Turn in the raw edges at each end, and slipstitch to neaten.

Fig. 169 *Joining fabric to make a fabric bow tie-back*

W.S.

(3)   Decorate the edges of the strip with narrow
       ribbon or other trimming and sew on a strong
       curtain ring at the centre back of the fabric
       length (*fig. 170*). Place round the curtain and
       tie into a bow. Hook the ring onto a cleat or
       hook at the side edge of the curtain.

Fig. 170 *Sewing a curtain ring to the centre back of the fabric*

Simple curtain treatment.

14
Decorative Edges for Curtains and Blinds

Decorative Borders

These are attractive when applied to the leading edges of curtains and along their lower edges. They can vary in width from 5–10 cm (2–4 in) and can be used very effectively on both short and full-length curtains (*fig. 171*).

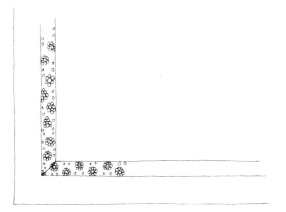

Fig. 171 *Decorative border applied to the leading and lower edges of a curtain*

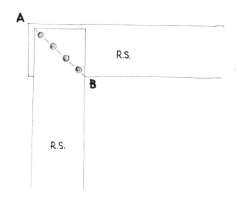

Fig. 172 *Making tailor tacks on a border*

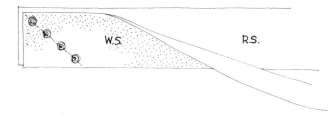

Fig. 173 *Tacking the border along the tailor tacking line*

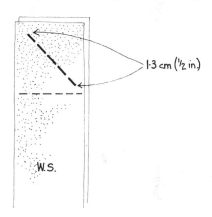

Fig. 174 *Machine line, leaving ends open 1.3 cm (½ in)*

To make and apply a border:

(1)   Cut strips of fabric equal in width and overlap them at right angles, making a line of tailor tacks from A to B (*fig. 172*). Cut tacks.

(2)   Place the right sides together and pin and tack along the tailor tacking line (*fig. 173*). Machine along this line leaving the seam open 1.3 cm (½ in) at each end to enable the edges of the border to be folded in (*fig. 174*). Trim the seam to 1.3 cm (½ in) and press open.

(3)   Turn under and press 1.3 cm (½ in) along the two raw edges of the border and apply to the curtain, valance, etc. (*fig. 175*).

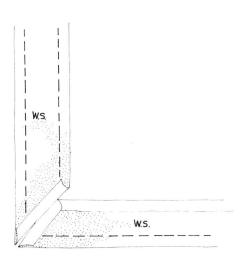

Fig. 175 *Turning in the edges of the border 1.3 cm (½ in)*

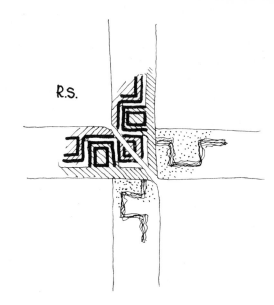

Fig. 177 *Mitring the corners and matching the pattern on a furnishing braid*

Fig. 176 *Making a wide border in a plain fabric in order to adapt curtains to fit a different window*

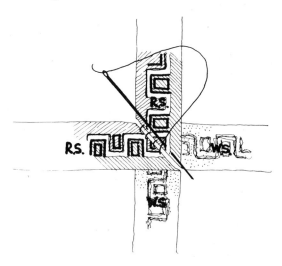

Fig. 178 *Braid folded to form mitre and slip tacked on the right side*

Wider borders of contrasting or different fabric can be made in the same way and let into curtains in order to lengthen them or make them wider. This is a useful way of adapting curtains to make them fit a different window (*fig. 176*).

Braids and Trimmings

Decorative braids and trimmings on curtains, pelmets, blinds, etc., are usually applied parallel to a straight edge. It is often necessary to mitre the corners, and if the pattern is very obvious it should be matched if possible.

To mitre a braid:

(1) Take two lengths of the braid or trimming of equal width and fold them at right angles taking care to form the mitre at an angle of 45° (*fig. 177*). Press. Slip tack the two folds together on the right side (*fig. 178*).

(2) Stitch along the tacking line on the wrong side. Trim seams and press flat. Neaten raw edges by oversewing (*fig. 179*).

To apply a decorative braid:

This can be applied to a curtain with or without a

wadded edge (*see page 52*). When a curtain has a wadded edge the braid should be stitched in position on a line to correspond with the finished width of the wad, i.e. 6.4–7.5 cm (2½–3 in) from the edge of the finished curtain. The braid is sewn to the curtain before applying the lining and the heading.

(1) For a curtain without a wadded edge tack a guide line 6.4–7.5 cm (2½–3 in) in from the finished edge of the curtain at sides and lower edge (*fig. 180*). When trimming a curtain with a wadded edge make the tacking line at the same time as making the wadded edge (*see page 52*).

(2) Tack the braid or trimming to this guide line on the right side of the fabric. Sew into position using small running stitches positioned 3 mm ($\frac{1}{8}$ in) from the outer edges of the braid (*fig. 181*). Take care not to pull the stitches too tightly as this can make the braid pucker. Mitre the corners as above.

Decorative Furnishing Cord

Furnishing cord is made up of three or four thick cotton or silk strands twisted together, and is similar in appearance to piping cord. It can be used effectively to decorate curtains, pelmets, roller blinds, etc., when a less costly trimming is needed. As it is often applied to the edge of a curtain or blind it cannot be tacked on first, so extra care is needed when sewing it.

(1) Bind the end of the cord with thread to prevent its unravelling.

(2) With the right side of the fabric facing, place the cord onto the edge of the fabric, holding it with the left hand.

(3) Pick up 3mm ($\frac{1}{8}$ in) on the fold of the fabric and insert the needle behind three strands of the cord. Take the needle back again into the fold and continue stitching (*figs 182 and 183*). When reaching a corner, twist the cord slightly to enable a neat turn to be made. Before finishing off, tie the ends of the cord in two places and cut in between them. This prevents the cord unravelling too much.

(4) To finish off, take the cord to the wrong side of the curtain or pelmet and position under the lining. Unravel the cord and stitch down the strands neatly.

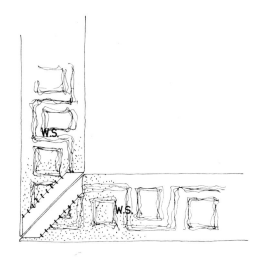

Fig. 179 *Oversewing the braid to neaten the seam*

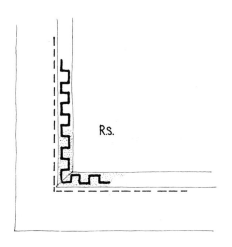

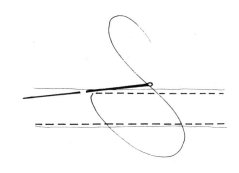

Figs 180 and 181 *Applying braid on a tacking guide line*

109

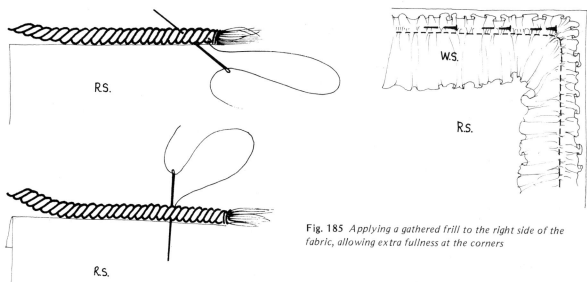

Fig. 185 *Applying a gathered frill to the right side of the fabric, allowing extra fullness at the corners*

Figs 182 and 183 *Applying a decorative cord*

Ric Rac Braids

Wide width ric rac braid can be obtained in many colours and is an attractive trimming for curtains and blinds made from light furnishing cottons and ginghams. It should be tacked into position on the right side of the fabric and then either machine or hand stitched into position. It can be stitched by hand using an embroidery thread and couching stitch (*fig. 184*), which makes a very decorative finish.

Fig. 184 *Applying a ric rac braid*

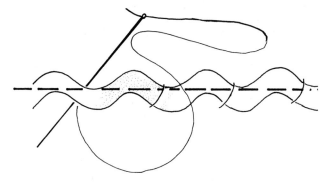

Frills

A gathered or pleated frill can be used effectively to decorate the edges of curtains, pelmets, tie-backs, blinds, etc. The frill varies in width according to the item being trimmed. Narrow frills are usually made from double fabric.

Gathered frill

(1) To make a 7.5 cm (3 in) frill cut a piece of fabric one and a half to two times the length of the edge to be frilled, if necessary joining the fabric pieces.

(2) If making a continuous frill, e.g. for a curtain tie-back, join the short edges of the strip together, fold and press in half lengthwise and make two rows of gathering stitches 6 mm (¼ in) from the raw edges. If a long frill is being made, divide the strip into sections. This prevents the threads breaking and enables the gathers to be evenly distributed.

(3) With right sides together, pin and tack the frill to the fabric being trimmed and arrange the gathers evenly, but allowing slightly more fullness at any corners there may be (*fig. 185*). Tack and machine into position.

Pleated frill

(1) Cut out and prepare the strips of fabric as for the gathered frill but allow three times the length if making knife or box pleats without a space between.

110

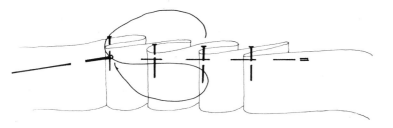

Fig. 186 *Making a knife-pleated frill*

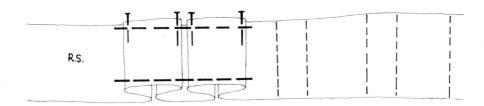

R.S.

Fig. 187 *Making a box-pleated frill*

(2) Pin into pleats, measuring accurately (*figs. 186 and 187*). Tack and press.

(3) Make two rows of machine stitching 6 mm (¼ in) from the raw edges to hold the pleats into position. Apply to the fabric as for the gathered frill.

Covering Piping Cord and Cutting on the Cross

Use strips of fabric cut on the bias or cross grain of the material to cover cotton or synthetic piping cord. This makes a smart decorative edge for pelmets, blinds, curtain tie-backs, etc. It has many uses when making soft furnishings for the home.

Piping cord can be obtained in several different thicknesses. Choose from fine, medium or coarse, depending on the item being decorated. Cotton piping should be carefully shrunk before use; otherwise, when washed or dry cleaned it will shrink and the strips of fabric covering it will pucker. Most cord is sold as shrink resistant, but if no guarantee is given, shrink it by boiling it for five minutes in a saucepan of water, drying it thoroughly before use.

Fabric cut on the cross has more 'give' and is much more flexible than that cut on the straight of the grain. This makes it easier to apply to a curved edge, as it moulds well and sets properly. To be really successful it must always be cut on the true bias or cross of the fabric.

The strips used for covering a decorative piping cord show up best in fabrics that contrast well with the item being decorated. However, try to match weights and textures of fabrics for the best results.

Cutting fabric on the cross

(1) Fold the material diagonally so that the selvedge thread lies across the crossways thread, i.e. the warp across the weft (*fig. 188*). Press. Cut along the fold. The material is then on the true bias or cross grain.

(2) In order to make all the strips exactly the same size, make a ruler in stiff card 3.8 cm (1½ in) wide to use as a guide. This is the most usual size of strip used for soft furnishings but a wider ruler 5 cm (2 in) wide could be used when covering the thicker piping cords.

(3) Place the edge of the ruler to the cut edge of the fabric and mark with a sharp piece of tailor's chalk, making parallel lines the same width. Cut along the lines and continue until sufficient strips have been made (*fig. 189*).

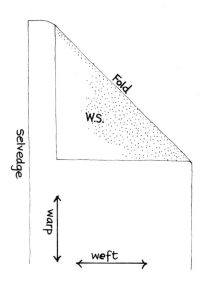

Fig. 188 *Folding fabric to make crossway strips*

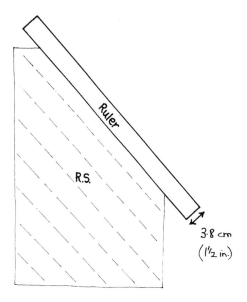

Fig. 189 *Marking out the fabric using a rigid ruler*

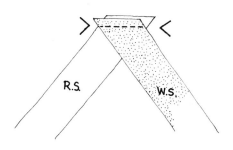

Fig. 190 *Joining crossway strips on the straight grain*

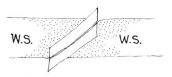

Fig. 191 *The join pressed open*

Joining crossway strip

Joining crossway strip

All joins made on crossway strips should be made on the straight grain of the fabric. Place two strips together with right sides facing and pin and stitch the seam, making sure that the strips form an angle as shown in fig. 190. Press the seam open and trim away the ends (*fig. 191*).

Quick method of cutting on the cross

When several lengths of crossway strips are required it is useful to be able to prepare them without having to join each strip separately. The following simple method can save much time:

(1) Take a strip of fabric 23 cm (9 in) wide. The length of the strip should be at least twice the width, i.e. 45.5 cm (18 in) or more.

(2) Fold over the top right-hand corner to obtain the direct cross (*fig. 192*). Cut off this corner and join to the lower edge with a 6 mm (¼ in) seam (*fig. 193*). By adding this piece, no fabric is wasted.

(3) With a ruler 3.8–5 cm (1½–2 in) wide, mark lines on the right side of the fabric with a sharp piece of tailor's chalk, parallel to the top edge. Mark also a 6 mm (¼ in) seam allowance down each side and mark the first and second line A and B as in fig. 194.

(4) Put a pin through the wrong side of the fabric at point A and take it across to point B, pinning very accurately with right sides together. Continue pinning along the seam. Tack and stitch the seam, checking first that the lines match up exactly. This makes a tube. Press seam open.

112

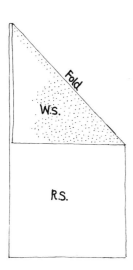

Fig. 192 *Folding the fabric for the quick method of cutting on the cross*

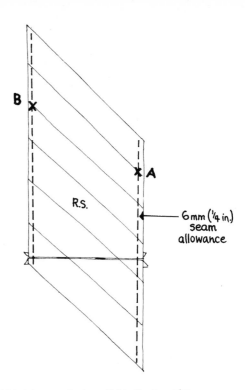

Fig. 194 *Lines marked parallel to the top edge*

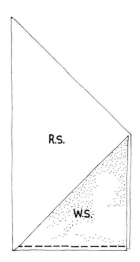

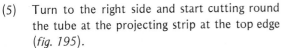

Fig. 193 *Joining the cut off corner to the lower edge*

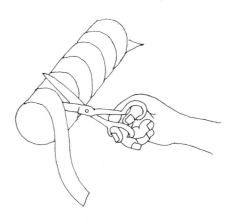

Fig. 195 *Cutting round the tube to make a continuous length of crossway strip*

(5)   Turn to the right side and start cutting round the tube at the projecting strip at the top edge (*fig. 195*).

A length of 23 cm (¼ yd) of fabric 91.5 cm (36 in) wide makes approximately 5 meters (5½ yds) of crossway strip 3.8 cm (1½ in) wide.

If larger pieces of fabric are available the top right-hand corner and the bottom left-hand corner can be cut off and set aside. This produces the same shaped piece of fabric but has the advantage of having fewer joins in the tube. Remember that the length of the strip of fabric must be at least twice the width (*fig. 196*).

Square pieces of fabric can also be utilized in a similar way by cutting and joining as in figs 197 and 198, placing AB to CD with right sides together.

113

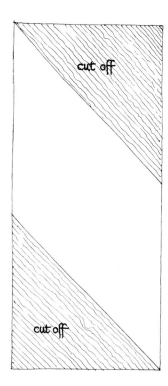

Fig. 196 *Alternative method of cutting, using a longer, wider strip of fabric*

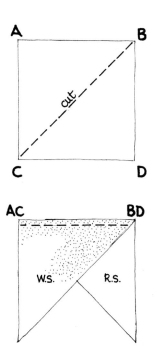

Figs 197 and 198 *Using a square piece of fabric*

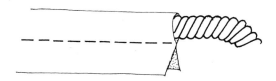

Fig. 199 *Tacking the fabric strip over the piping cord*

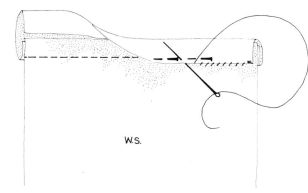

W.S.

Fig. 200 *Making a bound edge*

Applying the piping cord

Fold the strip in half lengthways and insert the piping cord. Tack and stitch the cord into position and apply to the curtain, pelmet, etc. (*fig. 199*). When applying piping to a curved edge clip the crossway to enable it to mould to the shape required.

Bound Edge

A bound edge can be used successfully for the edges of frills, tie-backs, valances, etc., and should be cut on the bias or cross grain of the fabric. Cut the strip three times the required finished width. Usually, a strip 3.8–5 cm (1½–2 in) is wide enough.

(1)   Prepare strips of fabric using the method described on page 111 or if large quantities are needed use the quick method of cutting. Remember to join the strips together on the straight of the grain (*fig. 190*).

(2)   Place the edge of the crossway strip to the right side of the edge to be bound. Tack and machine 1.3 cm (½ in) from the raw edges (*fig. 200*).

(3)   Turn the strip to the wrong side and fold in 1.3 cm (½ in). Pin and tack so that the fold comes onto the line of machine stitching. Hem by hand so that the stitches are worked on the machine line (*fig. 200*).

Metric conversion table

in	cm	in	cm	in	cm
$\frac{1}{8}$	3 mm	8½	21.5	23	58.5
¼	6 mm	9	23.0	24	61.0
½	1.3 cm	9½	24.0	25	63.5
$\frac{3}{8}$	10 mm	10	25.5	26	66.0
¾	1.9 cm	10½	26.5	27	68.5
1	2.5	11	28.0	28	71.0
1¼	3.2	11½	29.0	29	73.5
1½	3.8	12	30.5	30	76.0
2	5.0	12½	31.5	31	78.5
2½	6.4	13	33.0	32	81.5
3	7.5	13½	34.5	33	84.0
3½	9.0	14	35.5	34	86.5
4	10.0	14½	37.0	35	89.0
4½	11.5	15	38.0	36	91.5
5	12.5	16	40.5	37	94.0
5½	14.0	17	43.0	38	96.5
6	15.0	18	45.5	39	99.0
6½	16.5	19	48.5	40	101.5
7	18.0	20	51.0		
7½	19.0	21	53.5	48	122.0
8	20.5	22	56.0	54	137.0

Glossary of British Terms and their American Counterparts

Buckram—a coarse fabric of cotton or linen that can be used for stiffening pelmets

Bump—coarse fabric or matting used for interlining curtains

Calico—unbleached muslin

Crossway strip—bias strip. A strip of fabric cut across the weft and the warp of the fabric

Domette—baize or coarse flannel in which the warp is cotton and the filling woollen. Used for interlining curtains

Felt—a non-woven fabric that does not fray

Heading—top edge of a curtain from which the curtain is hung

Lining sateen—closely woven cotton fabric with a shiny surface used for lining curtains

Meter stick—yardstick

Pelmet—fixture at the head of the curtains that conceals the tracks and fittings

Rep—transversely corded or ribbed fabric

Roller blinds—window shades

Selvedge—the edges of a woven fabric running parallel to the warp

Tacking cotton—basting thread

Template—a pattern used as a guide when cutting out

Turnings—seam allowance

Valance—pleated or gathered piece of fabric used at the top of a curtain. Can also be used to describe fabric fitted under the mattress to conceal the base of the bed

Velcro—a touch-and-close fastening. One side of the tape is covered with a nylon fuzz and the other with tiny nylon hooks which catch on to the fuzz when the two surfaces are pressed together

Vilene—bonded fabric used for interfacing

Wadding—batting or filling

List of Suppliers

United Kingdom

John Lewis
Oxford Street
London W1 and branches
Furnishing fabrics, shower curtain fabric. Roller blind kits and fabric. Curtain tracks, poles, fittings and accessories. Interlinings, interfacing and buckram.

Distinctive Trimmings
11 Marylebone Lane
London W1
and
17 Church Street
London W8
Trimmings and accessories for curtains and blinds.

Laura Ashley
183 Sloane Street
London W1 and branches
Fabrics and trimmings.

Sanderson & Son Ltd
Berners Street
London W1
Furnishing fabrics.

Descamps
197 Sloane Street
London W1
Furnishing fabrics.

McCullach & Wallis Ltd
25—26 New Bond Street
London W1
Haberdashery, linings and interlinings.

Habitat Shops
Roller blind kits. Furnishing fabrics.

The Felt and Hessian Shop
34 Greville Street
London EC1
Felt and hessian in a wide range of colours.

Kirsch (Antiference) Ltd
Bicester Road
Aylesbury, Bucks.
Curtain tracks and poles. Fittings and accessories.

Graber-Marvic Textiles Ltd
41—42 Berners Street
London W1
Curtain tracks, poles and accessories. Fabrics and trimmings.

Rufflette Ltd
Sharston Road
Wythenshawe
Manchester
Tracks, poles and fittings. Accessories, trimmings, tapes.

United States of America

American Handicrafts
2617 W Seventh Street
Fort Worth
Texas 76707

Economy Handicrafts
50-21 69th Street
Woodside
New York 11377

Lee Wards
Elgin
Illinois 60120

Peters Valley Craftsmen
Layton
New Jersey 07851

Kirsch Co.
Sturgis
M1 49091

Chain Stores:
    Ben Franklin Stores
    Jefferson Stores
    Kay Mart
    M. H. Lamston
    The May Co.
    Neisners
    J. C. Penny Stores
    Sears Roebuck
    Two Guys
    Woolworths

The Counting House at the Hammock Shop
Box 155
Pawleys Island
So. Carolina 29585

Velcro International Ltd.
681 Fifth Avenue
New York 10022

A directory of specialist suppliers, *Where to Get What*, is published by Penland School of Handicraft, Penland, New Carolina.

Index